THE DARK
DANCE

❖ ⟶ OF ⟵ ❖

TIMES

OLIVIA CONDE

author HOUSE®

AuthorHouse™ UK
1663 Liberty Drive
Bloomington, IN 47403 USA
www.authorhouse.co.uk
Phone: UK TFN: 0800 0148641 (Toll Free inside the UK)
*   UK Local: (02) 0369 56322 (+44 20 3695 6322 from outside the UK)*

Published by AuthorHouse 03/10/2022

ISBN: 978-1-6655-9686-2 (sc)
ISBN: 978-1-6655-9687-9 (e)

Contents

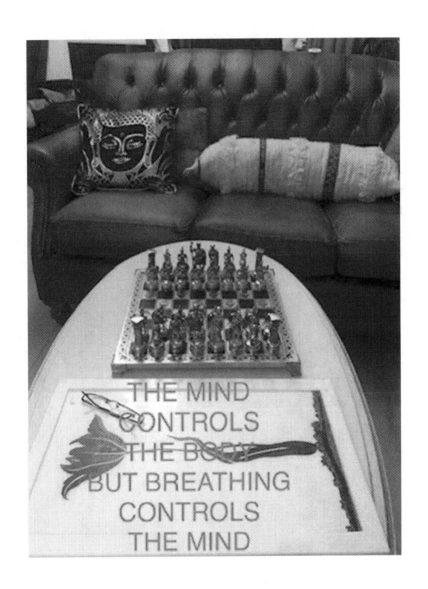

Poems of The Universe

The symbolic reproduction process is the dark dance of times.

Losing the north, a vertiginous abyss sucks up the roots.

The population abandons its vague loyalty by selling its fears to enemies of power.

There are principles and values that are only in content.

Everyone talks about peace but marginalization is for competitions.

Reading between the lines may reveal hidden answers.

Trampoline footprints have centuries of approval.

Trade barriers with stepping stones.

Name changes from the elite are hoaxes to distract the public.

There are leaders who are controlled puppets.

Mass mental studies are among top secret meetings.

The reincarnation of crosses are the modern Illuminati.

The robotic force can lead humanity to the demise.

Voices make decisions for behavioral performances

1   Princess Lady Diana

Like a warm swan she sailed across the ocean,
In her captive smile with love flooded life,
Among his sweet image, smiles of a child were scattered,
With fantastic amusement his mood grew bright,
An attractive star thrown on an abysmal journey,
Between baptism of fire the natural flourished in the jungle,
Outside palace walls watch unseen eyes,
Around mixed stories sound with amazement,
Charming public struggles leave legacies,
With its warm humanity it is discovered adorable to wake up,
Where submerged footprints leave glances with sighs,
Under a curtain of Valleys hidden clumsiness descended,
Some lights go out between mean customs,
Between sad explosions roots flowed in songs,
They were the gleams of dawn left by their descendants,
The industry of decency loses the north senseless,
Between bitter persecutions tears fall without shouting,
Boundaries cross barriers between pain leave furies,
With royal freedom a new experiment is born,
A passage of campaigns leaves a luminous power,
A comforting wind remains on defeated backs,
The sun watches through the clouds the footsteps of fallen rain,
The last call rings with a brief greeting says goodbye,
The obelisk was sealed in the Egyptian sphinx,
The manifestation resounded in the temple of energies,
Fluorescent sirens announce with astonishment the lost,
The distance with the nearness will let the earthquake rest,
The garden promenade becomes a sea of flowers,
They leave cold horseshoes sounds of hidden footprints.

2 The All-Seeing Eye

A septa between rituals for those who talk too much,
Owl eyes handing the baton to the next side,
The trained red brigades hand over their passports,
Borders are divided to put beings against others,
Thought without control reaps the storm,
Our imaginable fable is the factory of the future,
The echo chained to what should not be will live in sacrifice,
They are the elevated brotherhood from other more planets,
Intervening in dominating other energies are nurtured,
The hour of reason is to live in constant acceptance,
While the capacity is implanted the evolution is controlled,
Developmentally challenged thinking ability is destroyed,
Mind controlled controlling own progress,
The rat line joins the costume squad,
The serpent priest leaves tracks and traps,
The laughing black rose sits to watch on,
The thunder eagle triumphing among sad crosses,
The brotherhood of the pyramid sees everything from the dome,
The pantheon bends with rays of synchronized clocks,
The pillars of the sun let down gods of power to earth,
The phoenix was joining the solar energy of the model,
The Child of the dark moon is already easily controlled,
A robot enters and orders with abstract thoughts,
The priests are a privileged manipulator vehicle,
The rebirth of the triangle is the essence of power.
The pyramid is the continuation of the corner that generates,
The spy who works in the shadows lulls the people to sleep,
They watch between their best ally in the night and their enemy
in the day,
The plan is to know how to use the formula so that the human forgets.

3 Masquerade Balls

An exoteric federation in the hands of few men,
A temple of black magicians with an enteric symbol,
Between the cross and the hammer a hermetic fire will burn,
Servers should be few and kept secret,
Dark forces must castrate thoughts of peoples,
Compassion is the vice of kings crushing the unhappy,
Attacking each other among wretches is the battle of conquest,
Servants of wrathful gods seek worship,
Compassion does not exist only dance is spears and swords,
Sacrifices and tortures are called of ancient lusts,
The prison wardens feed on pain,
The power of flowers does not lose its irony between corners,
The battle is control to trample the heathen,
A torment trapped between demons becomes a prophecy,
The power to charm audiences is in the vibration,
Odin's runes mark the symbols of pillars,
Some actors act and other scripts are prepared,
When climbing the sphere thirteen steps mark restrictions,
Some arcanes draw secret signs in a game,
On the horizon some white horsemen disguise themselves,
Footprints riding tend to convince,
Drugs and terrorism words of primordial weaponry,
A camouflaged invasion stimulates outbursts,
Challenges and doubts are calmed with additive antidotes,
By disabling disagreements the mind cries in silence,
Raising dominate each other nurtures Loneliness,
To undermine weakness false drug wars are born,
The war machine is a world game plan,
The racket of the good game is disguised as freedom.

4   Tribe of Lineages

The web legacy absorbs the traces of cracks,
The sect devours the cries between dark corners,
A transformed paradise knowing what the objective is,
A light blue box is an antidote to persecution,
Skull and Bones Society is the invisible hand,
Black organizations prepare suicide brakes,
The sovereign clan is the hidden order of throats,
Campaigns of thieves are protected with torches,
The CIA lowers its head to continue on the clean list,
Lineage of the phoenix is on the white list but it is red,
Expert codes are Swedish felled trees,
The united tyranny trains itself on infiltrated excuses,
Lineages become fire of rituals and sacrifices,
In a bonfire spirits are charred with debates,
Browsing freely dark smiles open in tribes,
The inheritances leave cycles in magnetism of attraction,
The mystery schools are ancient from reptiles,
Pharaohs became puppets in scarlet hands,
Initiated servants are slaves of municipal councils,
The circuit board an energetic receiver and transmitter,
The global clavicle tablet surrounds crops with hieroglyphs,
The Lion of power sealed in recognized sacred temples,
The red cross of Saint George sacred symbol of victories,
The spiral lines of intersect renewable energies,
From Stonehenge to the Grand Canyon look,
An astronomical clock leaves traces for encounters,
The Phoenix bird an emblematic symbol for sun worship,
Phoenician navigators rely on ethnic groups,
Where the Danube dragged the foundation conquests.

5 Addicted Ceremonies

The dogmas are the carcinogenic bands without control,
A war becomes a banquet for missions,
The receiver of the rebellion is clothed by currents,
The accelerated balance is in vibration by energies,
Other entities are capable of reducing bodies,
Sacrifices with pressure are joined with recognition,
A desert imbalance is chained to paradise,
The dangerous game delta target is cautiously added,
The magnetic layer is very separated by consciousness,
The belief in victimhood is punishment with imbalance,
The fire club takes levels to found separation,
The prison guards are the vehicle of the process,
There are opposing dogmas with logistic brotherhood,
The unbalanced collective mind reinforces the ceremonies,
When you lose confidence in yourself, the devil approaches,
By giving up the right to think, the end is to kill and die,
Mind control experiments become cults,
The dark mysteries deal with drugs to manipulate,
Demonic possessions are ancient experiments,
The monarch project is one of the suckers to alter,
Orphaned eyes wander around waiting to be used,
Multiple personalities have many compartments,
Children abused while authorities look the other way,
The monarch butterfly instructs to observe ashen,
Soldiers are trained to obey without question,
The slave camp has no exit voice,
A playground hides the satanic footprints.
The hymns sing while the temples murder,
The owl of the full moon each month marks the cracks.

6   The Blood Clock

The game of the squid more resistant than cockroaches,
The paper house will be monitored 24 hours a day,
The symbols mark rules with free decisions,
The masked men direct elections by voting,
For addicted needs returnees play along,
Watchers inject plans with absorbing fate,
The price of progress increases by defeating allies,
Without honor the rules are crossed without feelings,
The elegant suits are seen among the rubble,
The duels end in an attack to be picked up,
The hunger game is addicted tasty intrigue,
Some private rooms keep old rules,
On the other side of walls there are intruders gambling,
Some infiltrators have fun with pending plans,
Some lights go out to betray the heroes,
Among the covered ocean escapes are very few,
The prison island itself uncontrolled are unknown,
Revenge is made sweet by numerical loot,
Between the sword and the wall there are no legal flags,
Values are destroyed by undergoing the process,
Renunciations are issues in lonely corners,
Between tired looks the traces leave scars,
Between lost memories some tears hide,
Memories sleep that burn unhurriedly to challenges,
A dark tale finds the nightmares awake,
Declarations become macabre amusements,
Where the end of needles stops the clock of blood,
Looking straight ahead is optional to leave the past,
By not getting on the plane, revenge remains pending.

7 The Traces of The Past

The black nobility from curtains with distractions,
Between disguises of towns with few alternatives,
Spies ambassadors passing plans to the Jesuit,
The huge empire of power from Venice and the Vatican,
Among trade routes with pagan traditions,
A star of alliances with sinister traditions,
The Babylonian brotherhood with bloodlines incorporated,
The Lion roars with distractions to reinforce the story,
Maritime transport based on control and trade,
Where in the key point the change of cultures intervenes,
Minting one's own coins for power and challenges,
Victims oppressed by the mentality of oligarchies,
Between alliances and wars impositions are debts,
The sale of bonds getting out of control is destruction,
The dynasties of control radically change rules,
Conditions must be adapted to the roots of control,
Several projects are paralyzed due to the danger of competitions,
The octopus of power absorbs all competitors,
Rich bankers managing the bond foundation,
The federal reserve is created with bank benefits,
The sovereign currency created to indebt the world,
Where the printing presses themselves issue federal debt,
Where creative history sails a ship without doors,
A distant ocean leaves waves in favor of the hidden system,
Where is the national economic control is the surprise,
Suspicions are hidden between secret smiles,
The apparent liberation of humanity is in the union,
Plato's rebirth was a shadow against the wall,
The French Enlightenment gave rise to free expression.

8 The Power of Possession

Good and bad vision are traces with shades of gray,
Some scales left the Holy Spirit as symbols,
YuAn aphrodisiac fish crossed the heart of the castes,
A dove returned carrying an olive branch,
Some reptilian lineages return to the field of origin,
Worship architecture returns after the flood,
The Flower of Liz sealed symbol of the Babylonian Trinity,
The diadem of the monarchs symbolizing authority,
The branch-bearing brotherhood is the royal hierarchy,
Three devil horns are the divinity of power,
The white albino titans of the Hermesdeities,
Sinn Fein rituals with the terrorist political wing,
The key to the door to heaven putting the beliefs,
The fisherman's ring representing the draconians,
Intermediaries surrounded by imposed societies,
Controlled impulses without favor will be damned,
The same tools will be used by successors,
Power must creep with entrenched will,
From priests, rabbis, Hindus and Islamists,
Cardó is the hinge used for the doors of heaven,
Pedro meaning the great interpreter of the elections,
Learned transferred enter the astrology of power,
The reptilian program requires human sacrifices,
The addition to the blood is part of the energetic benefit,
Cannibalism still belongs to people's struggles,
In tidal wave cultures the deities still remain,
Between rituals there are possessions of human bodies,
Vibrations are used to seize minds,
Greeting signals are recognition marks.

9 Chained

The old goddess of routine is part of democracy,
The round table created to coordinate handling,
Feeding fear controls the power of the people,
Many absent-minded puppets are used to dominate,
The combination of passages expands with teachings,
The Sumerian aristocracy deities of the same spirit,
The Phoenician Goddess Barati empress priestess of water,
The language of iron is symbolized in Britannia,
In covers of darkness esoteric arts hide,
The black hand is evaluated by bloodlines at the round table,
Centralized power directs the means of production,
The pawns of the game lend themselves to creating terrorists,
Monsters imitating equality are classic wars,
Behind the screen is the sun palace of Versailles,
The control of reigns acts in possession and distribution,
The throne watches the black sun among created enemies,
Modern slaves are the military guards,
The servants do not differentiate between the new man,
The priest and priestess control the structure,
Organized crime is the most important hierarchy,
The round table has its own cobweb suckers,
Tariff trade holds the Allied reins,
The third world is the staff of the black nobility,
The cross of the puppets directs votes for elections,
The goal of peace manipulates the maintenance of war,
NATO control is the dictatorship of the tribe,
The official system tune creates the errand boys,
Sacrifice in rituals has days in a necessary core,
Reclaiming childhood amnesia barriers begin to fall.

10 The Red Serpent

The black rose is concentrated in the elite of witchcraft,
The delta program is the brutality of mental horror,
The secret language has keys to venerate the elite,
The symbols are means to follow the union of the traced,
The fiery sun is chosen for few trapped heroes,
The figure of gods begins with the statue of liberty,
The torch is the most obvious signature of the brotherhood,
The thunder bird has its nest in thirteen signs,
The all-seeing pyramid is the thread of the inner name,
The great seal of the dollar is the reptilian mark of the Phoenix bird,
The double-headed eagle is the main shield,
The obelisk and the copula represent the sun and the moon,
Cleopatra's needle is the energy of rebirth,
The timeline is synchronized by pillars of control,
Between squares badges with rings surround the incubated,
The golden files become the manipulative magician,
Lunar dawn ceremonies are degrees of loyalty,
The twelve letters of the zodiac hide the secret thirteen,
The arcanes are the great secrets to see triumphs,
The cups, coins, clubs and arrows pursue legends,
The card joker travels with occult information,
Chess is the real esoteric game without limits of battles,
The light and dark mysteries in gridded riddles,
The praises echo with evangelical principles,
The masters of coronations cover world chambers,
Stones with pagan crosses save centers with pillows,
The dove of the ancient throne flies in the territory of the dragon,
The reptilian cascade moves the hungry economy,
From the Sumerian nobility founded the red serpent.

11 Steps to Blindness

The bright sun worshiped with invisible frequencies,
Hunting in forests between rituals by humans,
Toy soldiers fall into psychopathic nets,
Those who control the present control history
From education is the control of manipulation,
When giving rights we forget the contact with the heart,
Between doctrinaire contests there are reckless cruisers,
The future called time is limited in thought,
The occult for blindness brings the tribe to follow their lineage,
The abyss of tears is in the corner without haste,
Humanity gave up its mind and its responsibility,
The foundation of control is to activate fear without mercy,
The frauds end in amazement and continue their rhythm,
Bloodlines have sucker guilds around the world,
Blaming each other are footprints to follow the division,
The wave pattern is the attraction of what we receive,
Four points of the pagan cross is testament history,
From the shell the game is an apprenticeship to master,
Mental servitude is in prison for beliefs,
The challenge observes but does not face action to change,
The club of islands applies a poison in addictive dose,
Any imbalance with intentions projects a goal,
The elite retain extremely calculated means,
The hologram ring will start with microchips,
Where nanotechnology hides with the science it leads,
Secret disclosures are threatened with blocks,
The forbidden limit keeps traveling by never being detected,
The arrow of awakening awaits the lost prestige.

12 Spiritual Dimensions

Other worlds watch without sharing human arrogance,
Running away from things we don't want faces blockages,
This realm of illusion is manipulated by blind light,
The lower astral is directed by reptilian energies,
A leap of love waits for the connection of infinity,
The battle for land is still a wild life,
The lifting of the secret veil will rise from sleep,
The resonance is in awakening from a zero point,
Every man is just a breath awaiting wisdom,
The tunnel of the soul has balance and creativity with the moon,
Life is a fragile flame at any moment it goes out,
Time is passing for better and invest in the soul,
In eternity there is no end so don't run,
Resonance navigates the constellation of neurons,
Where the universe with its brilliance of lights attracts glances,
Stars with energies in the galaxy activate rebirth,
The infinite level of consciousness is an ocean of love,
Escaping from the spellbound cocoon opens up a new potential,
The connection is freedom of free and evolutionary expression,
The original source takes you beyond a leap of certainties,
The prison of conscience uses religion to lose glory,
There are micro antennas that surround frequency fields,
Positive emotions activate sleeping drops,
A hug is like a sound in a dose of abundance,
The heart chakra connects us to the infinite ocean,
The wheel of infinity has always sailed in life,
Where smiles are found there are doors to dimensions,
Spirituality is feeling part of the whole without obligations,
By keeping quiet you learn to listen and by listening you learn to
speak.

13 Health in Dependence

Science kills science, technology kills humanity.
The implants will be guardians to convert androids,
The final hours will be giving up the biological,
Convert from automation to apocalypse,
Voices make behaviors to act on decisions,
The hour of sacrifice implants pills with pneumonia,
Breath is restless with clogged additions,
Smiling and feigning sincerity everything is trapped,
Between lies we look at each other from the outside acting,
They put on the mask to become costumes,
Behind the truth hides the fear of breaking free,
In cowardice minds prefer to remain sedated,
Nothing matters as long as the deception works for dependency,
The lifetrap is the ghost of the human condition,
Between the true and the demonstrable there is always an abyss,
The search of science invites us to ignore other forms,
Experts just drag curtains on smoke signals,
So that between dreams the mind becomes blurry,
Where efforts turn into repeated doubts,
A monster dictates the board saying look but don't touch,
By conforming like puppets the wandering controlled magic,
Reason has no final judgment, only imbalance confuses,
An imperfect future is lived by looking for culprits,
Monkeys in suits begging for approval from others,
We are like rats for laboratory experiments,
A game so elegant that nobody knows where the enemies are,
There are no accidents, nothing happens without a reason.
Perception draws circles but never dominance,
The choice seems free but no one can see beyond it.

14 Holographic Bodies

The slave citizen is not invited to the party,
New social structure in a new era neohumanity,
A goal with hives in a collective brain,
The spark of reason does not act in the procedure,
A seed of change erases borders to go further,
Genetic improvement is to integrate cyberactivism,
The hybrid species will be Transhumance directed,
The differential equation is creativity of new application,
The alterations are imposed to continue dividing,
From human being to individual drawn to science,
The ultimate realization is to treat humans like machines,
The linear dictatorship without tears for the objective,
The disguise of science is to eradicate biological life,
Seeking perpetual immorality in cyberspace,
Unite the collective consciousness in a digital reality,
The apocalypse is visualized in the hivemind,
Where the giant intelligence joins the brain to the technology,
The real world will be the digital communication avatar,
Dreaming in life we float watching it go by in photocopies,
We turn the lie into the truth in order to survive,
Teleportation is the interconnected 3D worlds,
Where the values are forgotten to continue in the systems,
To evolve is to attribute a meaning to the whole,
It is an illusion to protect the prison in survival,
The human animal is a prisoner of his carnal instinct,
To get out of the kingdom of lies you have to erase beliefs,
In the goose razor the simple explanation is the most real,
When finishing a puzzle there are still essential pieces missing,
Going into the sunset without the sunrise programs.

15   Garnished Accounts

Debts sleep between decisions with nightmares,
The backdrop becomes the spy for secrets,
The perfect trap looks like a nice shelter,
In the meek sheep lives the wolf conquering the will,
Freedom of thought will become a sin,
Regimes penalize individuality with punishment,
With training supplies freedom is crushed,
Careful design controls the final behavior,
The chain of pleasure is a deluge of constant publicity,
Positive reinforcement leaves the will nullified without perceiving,
Between fear and pleasure is born the inclination to slavery,
A collective doctrine leads to not thinking for oneself,
The tyrannical divisions become doctrines with hatred,
Any different opinion is an oppressor for society,
The predator sets the watch for perfect security,
The pursuit of patrolling each other is a goal,
Accusing yourself with thoughts of moral obligation,
Harass yourself by refining self-censorship for submission,
Not giving an opinion puts the leader of the totalitarian power in victory,
When the sacrifice and effort is intolerable to the risk,
The kingdom of fanaticism creates bonds to calm threats,
The state resolves the addition between bread and imaginary circus,
Doing good is belief that you are doing something humanitarian,
Freedom is waiting in collective hypnosis,
The demolition is active but in the destruction phase,
The cage of the sleeping bird has the door open,
The goal is to remember how to fly again,
Time always waits only the value remains pending.

16   The Ritual of The Kingdom

You must not surrender to your dreams but to control,
A failure is someone who wants something but doesn't try.
The ruins are a gift and a path to transformation,
Everything will be lost in time like tears in rain
Time is the fire in which we burn towards a shooting star,
No one wins or loses the whole game is a distraction,
Coincidence does not exist, it is only a relationship with love and faith,
We never stop playing everything is measured on rails,
There are no winners or losers because they are only reflections,
Living in confusion repeating the same thing without realizing it,
A butterfly flaps its wings and causes a hurricane,
It is the abstract of thought that couples wonders,
Like the taste of a candy is there but it does not belong to us,
The destination connects and links with the next present,
From the womb to the grave we are united with others from the past,
The indecisive man interferes between mind and matter,
The special dimensions is that there are no limits,
Experience is a brutal teacher but you learn,
Standing still before an abyss can be productive,
Consciousness is not a journey out but in,
Do not look for answers in others, they are in you,
Near the sternum there is an open flower that drinks the honey,
No matter the paths chosen, they all lead to the same,
The one who thinks he knows himself well knows nothing,
Where you don't want to go is what must arise,
By embracing the pain of oneself you will win the game,
Far from the bitter world there is a place that gives rest,
Life without love is like a tree without color or fruit,
Hope is a good thing and good things never die.

17   The Art of Living

Life must be a pilgrimage quest,
Wishes swim and come out of trapped fish tanks,
Ghosts define the shadows of the sun in its rays,
The devil is the diamond of the game but nobody knows it
The last hiding place of an opponent is a quiet place,
In the factory of life there are times you lose your way,
Trusting in innocence one day the pieces come together,
A tree needs bad weather to lose its leaves.
Where the force of the storm performs the miracle of the sprout,
To get freedom you must first give it,
In the journey of the uncertain place there is happiness,
Evaluating our life positively is valuing that of others,
All in differences we have beauty in defects,
Finding the way means being free without anything written,
Freedom is on the other side of walls that one builds,
The universe does not waste anything, it only transforms it.
You cannot be forgotten because whoever loves you remembers you,
Death is the path we will all travel,
You can only take two paths, yours or the one someone else chooses,
Everything is in what surrounds us, it is only perceiving the formula,
The mind is a garden to cultivate your own palace,
Although there is drama you can contribute with a beautiful verse,
Life is the song of a bird flowing in mystery,
Childhood is the best meditation to meet again
Peaceful life begins where fear ends,
From a crystalline idea science is not debatable,
Reborn is an aroma with a constant celebration,
Maturity is being born again to feel the inner child,
Childhood is like background music in harmony.

18 The Lost Kingdom

The gold watch that makes you feel important is the shadow,
One day for its foundation and there is nothing left but ashes,
The scene of madmen pretends to be good with hatred and separation,
Humanity a plague of narcissistic parasites,
Between layers of paint and inside they are rotten,
A world built of fantasies among the synthetic,
Addicted pills between mind altering substances,
Controlling corruption with the motto of salvation,
The waters of the border with a magical wand,
Wars in the form of mind-altering advertising,
Brainwashed by mass media
Injectable needles with theories in social networks,
Digital numbers going up and down for catastrophes,
Excess information plagued in lunatic delusions,
Among the digital some puppets have gestures without movement,
A distant hill caught in corruption and revenge,
Between kindness cowardice seems civilized,
The limit of resistance is in the corner to survive,
In the absence of knowledge we think too much,
The feeling of dominance insists on playing god,
By forgetting the principles we attract everything that is conflictive,
Artificial intelligence will condition humanism,
The balance and imbalance walks in the challenge of the stumble,
On the tightrope there is a lesson between the sweet injustice,
Extinction in cruelty to plug broken holes in power,
The precipice approaches where oblivious to everything it destroys us,
Anxiety is the vertigo of feeling freedom to flow,
There are impulse decisions designed to hide,
Happiness is the best bubble to escape burdens.

19 The Enchanted Castle

The round towers aligned with the northern stars,
Missionaries found leather bags were bagpipes,
The Idris sculptures with coin stamps,
Oda Mussulman Gold dinar stamped in England,
The fore and aft Viking wing founding towns,
Agatha the lost city of Atlantis in Atlas Mountains,
The Isle of Man ancient class of the priestly Britannia,
The giant of Britannia crossed with serpent lineage,
The druidic mysteries wise men and sorcerers,
Men of sabers and oaks celebrating constellations,
Irish wizards of the titan Zeus with reptile lineage,
Oak men leaving teachings in caves,
Supreme authorities for spiritual healing,
Mistletoe and snake eggs solar energy attraction,
The sacred new and full moon in astrological ceremonies,
Celebration of the sun among groves seeking harmony,
Priests were doctors healing with magnetism,
Six levels by colors become reflections,
Teachings of learning in mysteries are hidden,
London and new Troy from Babylon guard portals,
There are alien cross origins with Draco bloodlines,
Martian cities from Mars conquering images,
The journey of the sun with zodiac signs circled from animals,
The levitate from mountains of the sun with reptilian schools,
Kabbalah from foundations chained to Masonic mysteries,
Esoteric torrent hidden between secret codes,
Infiltrated texts to promote manipulative dogmas,
Facade of gardens painting between fanatical feathers.

20 Psychiatrists that Enslave

The tornado comes and hits when it's unexpected,
Silent weapons put control with medication,
Mental evaluation enters through the supporting belief,
An accepted signature can be an eternal prison,
The pitfalls of the dark game are bureaucratized rules,
The cores of freedom are steps to obedience,
Controlled neurosis gives way to hidden power
There are shock troops infiltrated in public systems,
Manage way to way in case of alteration and complaints,
Control the direction of the world in favor of the government,
Organizations with similar programs are the design,
Incubate an operative for brainwashing,
Each level is still hidden in their jobs,
The society tunes the technique of imprisonments,
In distractions methods make believers,
The drug revolution chains minds,
The demand increases with the massive humanity,
Illustrated funds publish charity for further attack,
Global networks claim to be genuine groups,
Bombard reports with separate selections,
Controlling thought brings better rewards,
Creating a race of zombies is the key to brotherhood,
Traumas are used as bridges of obedience,
Homework is treated with addicted drugs to enslave,
The victim is programmed for a multiple disorder,
Doctors follow the cartel's rules of exploitation,
The connection of projects increasingly raises the barrier,
Solidarity madmen are programmed foroutrages,
Sleeping profits hidden with secret profiles.

21 The Magnetic Mountain

An internal clock with projected colossal magnetism,
Sunspot cycles are short and long,
Amazing and exact Mayan symbols were heritage,
The mediation of time tells ancient stories,
Consciousness throughout the solar system is mathematical,
Invisible frequency levels are nuclear effects,
Gigantic loops of fire with atomic radiation,
The iguana race with an internal clock synchronized to the sun,
The sages of Mars connect with current technology,
The sovereignty of the dragon is the physical heart of the solar system,
Smoke screens paralyze with separate religions,
Frequencies and vibrations affect the unconscious,
With the bombardment of laws the mental imposition is born,
Cloudy winds are decoded late,
Convincing are folk tales from history,
Bank dominance is the core for dictatorships,
The approach to jellyfish can paralyze us,
The thrill of winning turns the environment of success to losing,
A painting in clarity reflects a background without vision,
The temporary solution is distraction from the problem,
Modern indifference is the chain of excesses,
Entertainment is the exercise not to reflect,
The urgency of success looks to the sky with vague beliefs,
Excuses reveal tiredness trapped in cages,
The truth is a race looking for psychology heroes,
Fragile reality constantly feels accusations,
Survival repeats pleasant lies as keys,
The truth is mixed with paralysis from not being shared,
The perfect crime is not in not knowing, it is in not understanding.

From gold and silver are the old testaments,
All change in paper between clay to the recipient,
Only by moving a number precious metals disappear,
Systems that do not exist swallow properties that do,
The London branch protects the family empire,
Cleopatra's needle is related to pride,
The eagle with five arrows in its talons is the corporation,
The black nobility has the force behind the Normans,
Printing money without interest is federal reserve control,
When the monarchism falls, a new order is created,
Democracy is the best dictatorship for power,
Seeds of rebellion are sown with ancient methods,
The three-leaved plant contained in conspiracies,
The feet of the dragon are the imposition for fear and guilt,
Poverty is the grand ladder for darkness to climb,
Lunar society is true diplomacy for lies,
In the designed revolution there is no place for feelings,
False democracies rule and control freedom to think
The court of royalty is the hidden empire of the dragon,
The creation of the twelve stars leads to the thirteen,
With seven heads among seven days the seventh century begins,
Codes remain for passive distortion,
Logo geometries are guild creation,
Surrounding deities with twelve and six holy signs,
Seven golden candlesticks and seven trumpets all follow the rhythm,
With the apocalyptic continuation the seven dragons of fire,
In seven days the doves of the ark are sent as support,
Then follow the forty days with the healing mysteries,
With each frequency resonate numbers colors and sounds.

23 Coldness for Honor

The lion observes at the moment that the herd is distracted,
Reptilian schools have been for centuries as masters,
The six-pointed star creates the red shield,
The cross of salvation forms foundations with secrets,
Many charitable Baptists were mercenary bloodlines,
Causing wars is enough profit to create power,
The crowned heads have the structural dynasty,
The secret team approves missions to destabilize,
The invisible hand is an accomplice of the double cross,
Creating chronic stress is the perfect plan for psychosis,
The giant called the Internet assaults the mass mind,
The condition is to lose contact with reality,
The reign of ideological fanaticism draws ever closer,
Between desire and confusion they hail the government for security,
Opportunistically, the leader agitates the cloudy democracy,
The people seek reason but logic is already illogical,
In small periods of calm the tension rises to terror,
In moments of maximum tension, morale is destroyed,
Where power positions the solution as the only alternative,
The waves of terror make the individual beg for protection,
The loop for global manipulation is constantly repeated,
The oppressed oppressors become spies,
Cowards exercise complaints to continue in slavery,
Revenge becomes common by creating enemy groups,
Collective blindness ruins their very existence,
As the leader smiles watching the people submerge,
The wolf of the pack rests on the green grass,
To travel back you must double the experience.

Impulses are directed in a state of artificial consciousness,
The Masonic motto is Fraternity with Science Cell,
Unseen accomplices dragged into a trance,
The poor and marginalized multiply without justice,
Human rights almost do not exist for rational,
The repressive society is created by accomplices,
Reactions to govern go hand in hand with annihilation,
Unconscious intentions keep peoples asleep,
Taken into a trance they make us different from the real,
We live lethargic and focused on other people's visions Staying away focused on one's own vision,
We are in a time of adduced artificial consciousness,
A world of indifference is implanting systems,
Destruction falls before the eyes that do not want to look at it,
The human sheep predisposed to slavery,
Systems roar in desert alleys to obey,
Watching TV NEWS is a complete plan to submit,
Reproduction with the same name and size margined,
Compulsive purchases catch you without questioning your instinct,
Obedience to authority is restored in the foundations,
The structure is designed to write the next plane,
Two lanes in battle are for forced adaptation,
Some disappear to return in unsuspecting time,
Separate courts hide templar exploits,
The lunar association holds the key while opening the lock.

25 Change Linear Education

For prisoners the reference is the outside world,
In a cave a group of chained men shout,
They could only look at the bottom of the ancient cave of shadows,
Walls of disagreements entrenched in darkness,
The schemes of schools must be altered and reinterpreted,
The bureaucracy should turn around to feel freedom,
The task of education is a team solution,
Respect is the ability to accept the flow of life,
Obeying is not respecting when imposing a control,
Progress is to observe the methodology so as not to be obstacles,
The forest has the capacity with ancestral consciousness,
The mother satisfies the necessary structures without intervening.
Learning is a continuous transformation,
To die in beliefs is to be reborn in harmony,
The personal history that conditions traps the development,
A challenge to the unknown breaks educational repression,
The key to the essential is in the exercised example,
A teacher must be in a continuous change,
Doubts of ability mislead education,
To follow the instincts is to break the inertia of the scheme,
Get close to each other without fear of being caught,
Forget about competing for things that have no value,
Ask for opinions to know what we think and feel,
Experiencing dimensions are fruits for learning,
Enough of qualifying exams of imposing science,
It changes every time you decide to obey than to listen to you,
It changes every time you choose a goal instead of the route,
Change every time everything is the same to try something new,
Build visions for a new educational paradigm,
Making people feel and think is a new construction contribution,
Reality is not only looking at what is essential is transforming it.

26 Men of War

For the interest of possessions they instill innocent lives,
The seas hidden in enigmas become war,
The unconscious guard the layers of the interior,
There are collective masses between trapped cements,
Old wolves become fixed traces of instinct,
Some doors have cracks but they don't open.
In the back shouts of obey continue scratching his skin,
Some black sea trades one hell for the next,
Disguising in adoration escapes at the end of the road,
Being and not being becomes as real as submitting,
Between caves the winners carry the scars of losers,
Cannon noises leave permanent bolts of thunder,
The social fabric deteriorates over time,
Under a deluge of fire the mind is injected with rage,
Not all combat wounds are visible.
The burrow of escapes is eternal in history,
Farewell letters recording feelings,
The interior keeps the silence carrying the imposed plate,
The eyes dry tears between lonely emotions,
The steps are forced by the homeland with silent needles,
A food that poisons every day counts the hours,
Tiredness only continues until the waves calm down,
The soul asks for rest for a life of hope,
The darkness of the interior burns in bonfires of sparks,
They escape from everyone but they cannot escape from their interior,
The cure awaits where the anesthesia sowed an abyss,
A lonely star watches the no man's land,
Time remembers who you are not to the arrogance of power,
The little stay of the spirit goes lost in trenches.

27 The Goddess and The King

A serpent goddess has the head of a cobra,
With the intense hypnotic gaze to attract the prey,
Between lineages of rubble blue blood runs in the veins,
Looking for limb suckers in ashes they found,
Some kings were the dynasty of the sacred crocodile,
The great dragon observes monarchisms from Egypt,
Summits are extinguished between medallions of crosses,
Some bright faces reflected other members,
Observers chained the wandering monster,
A cruel criss-cross prince had a cloudy countenance,
Some abductees came down like fallen angels,
The punishing seraphim were thrown into an abyss,
An ancestral mother was tempted by vices,
In a chain of five points there were Martians,
Secrets were revealed to select humans,
Some fallen from the sky brought burning fragments,
The origin of the goat head is a spy goat,
Some observers tempted with the objective of controlling,
Some mask themselves with the image of kingdoms,
The possessed currents are by lineage genetics,
Hybrids carry human-like abductions,
The language of the apocalyptic book will let Jesus fall,
Some pharaohs seem Celestial Magic in their reign,
The force of the occult can travel beyond sound,
Clones are an important part of human development,
Thinking the impossible advanced societies appear,
Between rebirth and double cataclysm are reflected,
Seeking to become the members of the mental council,
In constant mystery royalty continues to implement rules.

28 Eclipse Nights

They blow calls at secret pact meetings,
Flood waters are restored with disturbances,
Mystery schools are rebuilt in lineages,
Magnate glances between priests and reptiles,
Dodging communication traps in hijacks,
The limitation is not uncertain only unlimited,
Opportunity is like a concentration camp,
The experience in victories turns into challenges,
A goal without concept with barriers without exits,
An owl watches the tracks of dark woods,
Where the mysteries of power play to dominate,
Fierce scales direct flags for trade,
The cold footsteps of guardians are wrapped with challenges,
Some encounters with the force forget the feelings,
The power of control encompasses macabre impulses,
Some cries link deaths to offering rituals,
Energies feed on poverty and suffering,
The chains sound in decades without limits to forgiveness,
Free fall is an order without right to claim,
Disappearances are part of sad news,
Searches are the theories to keep searching,
The beliefs of others are the most important part of the process,
Those who smile in the woods remain camouflaged,
Colors are not visible, bulbs break,
The echoes of darkness turn into bitterness,
In delusions fall the waves that vibrate in the environment,
The wind keeps the loads of bloody crosses,
The earth seals the steps in hard and dry leaves,
Time keeps waiting for the next free creation.

29 Cannibals of Summits

Grant evolutionary power to other alien entities,
The smoke room is formed in manipulated decrees,
The prison of the mind devours the right of perception,
Drugs calm the pressures of emotional pain,
Humanity gave up its mind and its responsibility,
The subconscious awaits the cleaning that the cesspool ruined,
On the surface a stifling heat seems illuminated,
The symbols of doctrines create religions to blame,
The sinister caverns restore the mass of farms,
Tornadoes are in the air and with ignorance they evade,
The elections are still in Martian threats,
Risk limits are too invisible to decide,
Since the ancient world the root follows the same structure,
The knot line continues to block the comfort zone,
The interlocking domain discusses how to divvy up the loot,
The challenges are keys to the origin of frequencies,
Doctrines are instructions with tangled silences,
The working sheep follows the path of the sleepwalking abyss,
The missing link is a murmur that disguises itself,
Genetic mixing is ancient knowledge,
The servants carry transplants to float recycled,
The fossils record the scheme of the inseminated source,
A recycling from the skies remained in the mountain atlas,
The brotherhood of lineages crosses without feelings,
Fierce rivals become lost pillars,
Dead sea battles translate cold floods,
North and south pole stars exchange visiting each other,
Great clouds with water boiled on the summits,
Facing darkness is the journey that tunes liberation.

30 | The Sun Temple

When a single virus shakes the domino comes and knocks down,
A vulnerable effect is enough to run systems,
Mystical powers in scientific rituals for the blind,
A distant future turns religion into science,
Innovations that thrill the sleeping masses,
Where order is suspended fantasy looks for another ghost,
The ray of rain opens a new temple for hailed,
Someone undressed observes distances without knowing the nearness,
Fierce abysses await the sun's chosen ones,
The novel image attracts sounding justified reality,
Where the loads weigh the addition lays its traps,
Values lose direction by submitting to what is foreign,
The authoritarian hierarchy invades decisive thoughts,
The obediences postulate marking intruders as kings,
Reason with doubt is trapped in fear,
A flash of smoke hypnotizes human free will,
Radiation begins with experiments for experiences,
The bursts become crystal balls for magic,
Finally they appear accused with criticism without evidence,
History becomes a gallery of horror between dreams and causes,
Crushing without quarter because the applause approves,
The noise of expression makes eternal submissive spectators,
Trading hope of happiness for panic and obsession,
Burning the world polarizes intrigued minds,
Fanaticism leads to doubling the effort when you forget,
Traumatized revolution puts goodness in the hands of power,
The motor of believers looks for culprits for not knowing each other,
A labyrinth is observed between dances without music,
The difference between seeing and being is the mirror image.

31 The Sacred Covenant

The reptilian heritage the great occult of the resplendent sun,
The future erased from the present wakes up separated,
In the north as in the south reason rises up without virtue,
A world regime with a digital look at movement,
The new scientist in dictatorship begins without looking back,
The exact species of trans humanism is without feelings,
The fanaticism with the demonic lineage is a consumerist,
The joke-less reptiles persistent in seeking terrorism,
Surrounded by lunatics they will watch each other.
The maniacs persist not to see independent beings,
Fear turns minds into obedient human resources,
By transmuting identity, reality is changed,
The line of fear creating in its paradigm producers,
In semi-darkness the necessary pressure is adjusted to the challenge,
The simulation lives in the true strategy of the pact,
The program is interested in covering all the data,
The architects of control tread snow without leaving a trace,
Putting loads is an ideal plan to be very busy,
The invisible prison is cautiously run to make addicts,
Raindrops are not heard even in storms,
It is a time of the dance of electronic images,
Swimming without distinguishing the true from the false,
Happiness delivered through a connected tube,
The old reality rests among the black swans,
The synthetic consumer industry is a great start,
The new route is the dimension of global trade,
An electric world united from distant nearness,
Clouds cross reality between the biological and the artificial,
Spirituality will be a formula for not dividing.

32 The Top that Smiles

The cannibal's bases protect their guardian limbs,
Controlling the masses like wolves their flocks,
The global creation with debts engulfs society,
Educational systems for unthinking slaves,
The Black Nobility performing between match games,
Voters open their mouths to applause the leader laughs,
The lights turn on sheep to participate in the circus,
The game tokens have an owner with adhered rules,
Surveillance will come under the skin with no way out,
The prescriptions imposed are for those born captive,
The prison leaves no explanations, it will only give opportunities,
Drugs are injected as genetic experiments,
The guardians of the treasure look faithful to the red shield,
The squires are clowns in the public comedy,
A technological tsunami will take control of minds,
The maniac system sets the target smoothly,
Servants enter heaven as Eden plans,
Selling climate change to feel like victims,
The tired rebel but still serve the monster,
The screams acclaim rights getting lost in the mists,
The stairs continue to receive taxes,
The passageways narrow clinging to illusions,
Breath grows cold watching discreet robberies,
The arrogant reserve rehearses songs with new couplets,
The receiving mirror receives the demanding pleas,
Living with cameras they respond to the program they need,
Invading markets always come out as winners,
Solar activity amazes with not very natural disasters,
The artificial exceeds the target in the target of destiny.

33 Burned Feelings

Careful steps mark the rules of the game,
The promise of sides sounds rational with education,
The returning world order offers a simple twist,
A salvation without logic appears as the miracle,
The traces are sealed where the top draws them,
Putting intruders the theory disguises itself unnoticed,
Recycling is constant in waves of a thousand colors,
The economy involves traps to erase properties,
A system of services calms ideas of possessions,
The ants do not observe until meteorites fall,
Power grows to control multiple immune heads,
The ship already has an insignia for the hidden target,
The owner of time separates beings to destroy them,
In an acceleration of dust some giants fall,
Turbulence is created for destabilization,
Silk specters between tricks devour each other,
A world without super powers is destined for the mechanical,
A latent fear lives for the worship of the monster,
On some lost rocks firmaments never end,
The witch hunt manifests old cultures,
Efforts lie unarmed in the prison of the system,
Routine is the illusion for constant stagnation,
Cities are giant machines to feel comfortable,
Entire civilizations fall silent between fables and comedies,
The price of errors observes scenes in terrible traumas,
The hive of customs is silent, memorizes and repeats,
Gazes at stars ask empty questions,
The closer the truth is, the better the lie,
Walking on the surface of the sun one forgets to look at the moon.

34 Erased Memories

The great black and white free do not remember colors,
The myth of Eden seeks the disobedient to obey,
The fury of the past guards a gallery of philosophers,
A declining cycle accelerates economic frustration,
A scale erases final symbols of civilized terms,
Diving into a better and worse line leads to divisions,
The suffocation of reality has no voice for changes,
Trusting others is like jumping into the abyss,
Understanding each other with a hug begins to fade,
The roots forget currents of identity for history,
To do with the currency taxes are born and the first beggars,
The tourism label paints a false support in cultures,
An incomplete identity created for frozen product,
Looking towards myths of the sky, fantasies are transformed,
Power justifies acts by putting on a cape of freedom,
The desire to exist is shown in public forlikes,
The watchmen themselves watch themselves thinking of gaining
power,
Resources fall with the economy that disturbs,
Reprehensible acts become unquestionable,
Life runs wild in the concrete jungle,
Flavors are forgotten to adapt to the synthetic,
When acclaiming security, submission is cultivated,
The fragile ego follows the master submerged by fear,
The sin of pleasure mixes with dictators,
The privileged are adored in the darkness of ceremonies,
The lies are covered with flowers regardless of aromas,
Between different classes with sacrifices are blinded,
Do not forget to open the window so as not to surrender to the future,
The truth only has one path and lies hundreds.

35 The Pill that Does

The holocaust of duty goes to a lonely society,
Removing responsibilities pleasures are implanted,
Disordered individually they are trapped in nostalgia,
The unattainable past hides a well of secrets,
By continuing in imitation, the realist identity is ignored,
One more product without aroma or time in the Resurrection,
Neon lights in a complex frozen eternity,
Pieces of reality turned into consumer goods,
Emotions fueled by shows that dope,
Times converted into a visual style of products,
Essences losing their aroma for replica copies,
Life invested only in earnings growth,
Swimming in seas without oceans or visible waters,
The collection of moments for inventory narration,
Expenditure figures regardless of the deep essence,
Lost aromas in the background of old movies,
Fleeing from the void, a melancholy chases the steps,
The adventurer with a virtual mission seeks connection,
Reservations are frozen waiting to see the changes,
Slowly by contamination they were prey to hunger,
A spiral viciously identifies the victims,
The triumphs return empty in the Tower of Babel,
Appearance to power is more compelled than being,
Loneliness faced with being attractive to sensations,
Routine looking to be special in labor competition,
Needing to deserve more regardless of others,
The relief project does not provide a solution without understanding,
In apparent stories they face invisible battles,
Fear of the unknown traps the weak in misery.

Putting the puzzle piece is different than inventing it,
The dreaming paradise envelops a fragile reality,
The crisis is mercilessly tearing apart the poor countries,
The government raises medals when it sees the obedient people,
The power of the shadow is the tool of transformation,
The will of the spider dictates the policy of the contract,
The sect operates legally without borders,
Between the walls, tyrannical globalised systems are recreated,
The ferocious dragon moves between discrete distances,
A new virtual securities code comes into force
The old human will be extinguished and replaced,
The implants subtly erase past systems,
Doors are perfectly invisible to the target,
Destabilisation furiously enters between oppressive crises,
The mentality of the herd in confusion will fall into the abyss,
The best control begins in communal enmity,
Development aid are pillars to create control,
Criticism is censored so as not to contradict norms,
Those who drown are saved to sink again,
Opponents are calmed in ghosts with delusions,
The virtual separates the biological with an artificial future,
The perfect genetic plan is to modify behavior,
Scientific engineering will force makeovers,
Christian civilization will sleep in memories,
Consumption and education will be dominated between barriers,
The new design with a perfectly interlocking end,
Accepting not knowing raises mountains to knowledge,
Learning to learn is the fragile reality of the beginning,
Man is the only animal that needs an owner.

37 Ecstasy that Provokes

Looking in the mirror is the first sign that surrounds us,
Everything like a diamond before it shines is coal,
The desire with fantasies in the interference of the hero,
If we didn't live for a purpose we wouldn't exist,
The struggle to live leads to transcend for memories,
Climb levels to reach different dimensional points,
Virtual scales that go beyond the physical imagination,
The age of information beyond knowledge,
The opinion in networks intrigues the existence in the world,
Remote Controlled Society In Ambush Temptation,
The time to think without processing wastes answers,
A blurry carousel spinning without brake gears,
A magnetic rhythm trapped in a vicious circle,
Life without evidence with prizes in empty titles,
Time of noise with fear where silence keeps rebellion,
Laboratory with multi ideas waiting for the solution,
Waiting for learning raining words of dictators,
Knowledge with answers without knowing the question,
Public opinions stain weakened emotions,
The cage of eternity is the dictatorship of pleasure,
The gear is still in the same puppet structure,
The ecstasy of consumerism leaves spaces far apart,
The infantilized world sees youth as eternal,
The play involves repeated sensations,
A market of relationships with tourist resemblance,
A pack of positive substances until emptied,
Battleships disappear as they spy on the quiet,
As tears in the rain join the great ocean,
The one is your unit of measurement as perhaps it is not.

38   Once Upon A Time

An old alarm awaits appointments for unfolding,
The time was precise, the eyes closed in seconds,
A soft wind seemed like an anesthetic injection,
Entering a dark window something coldwas intense,
In a jump I close my eyes where smiles catch me,
Some shadows envelop questions without answers,
In the search for something lost, an oblivion has doubts,
There are very blurred memories in the lost corners,
I can walk barefoot on some stones that burn
They change images very fast to take me to the abyss,
A sigh ignites with a dizzying fall,
The steps become sad with heavy illusions,
Back a flame looking for the riddle of fire,
Screams rise where ferocious lives sleep,
Across meadows a monster sits waiting,
The return of the past seeks to erase the wounds,
Breathing calms at the moment's awakening,
A woman was escaping from a nightmare that surrounds her,
The return continues when the night falls on the top,
Where the loads of the spy without memories weigh,
A hidden pain bears silent scars,
When running in the dream there is always the same look,
The doors are still closed when you cross empty,
Eclipses on each moon run through the hidden nights,
Bitter flavors want to turn into softness,
There are heartbeats that reflect the cracks in quicksand,
The waves of the sea blow in favor to take footprints,
The stars shine to be born again in your spirit,
The connection of forgiveness once upon a time of hate.

39 Dating Star

I will raise my throne where the world will listen attentively,
In the Mount of testimonies I will sit on the sides,
Among deities I will be similar by attraction of rituals,
As a master of light in the androgynous I will be invisible,
In the power of darkness they will acclaim my power,
Rituals for life among the hidden sun star,
Power is conquered by exchanging trust,
Civilization accepts and strengthens barbarities,
The aim of the agenda is to forget the rights and freedoms,
Science kills science, technology kills humanity.
Signs between words disturb from the ambitious elite,
In all foreign conspiracy with power there is no loyalty,
Double public figures are strategies for revelations,
Friars in black survive the order of force,
The black nobility follows prestige delicately,
Puritan families dominate the order of genetics,
The gentlemen of Malta are more than catholic aristocrats,
Fighting the rebellion is a well-coordinated bond,
Exclusive traits are attached outside the pyramid,
Native American Geronimo Apache his plundered grave,
The skull of the popular to use in evil rituals,
Careful spheres of selections are collected,
Only among secret members does the patriarchy continue,
The coordination of the elite is the society of revolution,
Members follow routine cues like an orchestra,
Eugenics from rituals is to confirm the organization,
On each side there are agents to continue control,
Giving up the right strengthens global networks,
The low levels are the light that lets the darkness grow.

40 Interior Forests

The secret forces are the discreet quicksand,
The believers of wars are butchers of massacres,
Human catastrophes are cannon fodder for order,
Costumes look proud with hidden designs,
Distractions with versions are altered in reports,
The false suicides are the formation of the system,
Every movie is a high command squad,
A good complete plan in classic silence reports,
One missing link method is the organized key,
All double crosses are threats to covert traps,
There are pawns in games that go unnoticed,
The guardians give up their ideas of expression,
The operation lowered the world calms everything with strategies,
Trance windows are prey to captivate memories,
Mental waves fixate on foreign eyes deeply,
The Rosa Cruces have no limits in their meetings,
When shaking hands the traces leave tremors,
Executions are covered with smiling betrayals,
The Templar Crusaders looking for a place in the sky,
The cosmic horror is in the unknown between doubts,
A concentration camp hides without tears,
Discipline is an obligation to walk with order,
Goals look blindly at growth,
Dogmas are organized in the form of new languages,
As you enter the forest there are wild cats in trees,
The dark inquisition controlled by monarchisms,
Parallel councilors serving no kingdom,
A state of blind rage took possession of weak bodies,
The cold forests in darkness leave waves without colors.

41 The Last Light Bulb

Safety by obedience is in doubt,
Robotic plans are the best strategy,
Vigilantes are assigned to wear disciplinary collars,
For survival to participate in security of the nation,
The reverse gear does not exist to return to the cave,
Synthetic genetics duplicates with reproductive technique,
The chain of revolutions is mixed with animals,
Cybernetic beings in steps indistinguishable from the human,
Conquest seeks immortality to survive
Peaceful dreams are written on Sumerian tablets,
In the arcanes of nature is the treasure of the gods,
Diving into astrology the symbols direct,
The crystal generation falls into the dragon's pit,
Where the ultimate plan is hidden is the target set,
A lost ray hibernates in the star constellation,
Under the ocean a continuous list in hidden bases,
The war sold as peace delivers the rules of the game,
The domino concentrates on the last tile quickly,
A program makes immutable laws of the starting point,
A timeless hit has no bounds link,
A cult without borders creating the global state,
The hunger game society depends on the submissive,
The firebird throws the leftovers for the last days,
The survivors will not remember the levels below,
When crossing sectors, thoughts are divided into glances,
The heart grows cold by losing the connection of love,
The society symbol focuses on needing an owner,
Private property no longer belongs to the people.

42 The Crystal Age

The age of comfort controlled by education,
The last organic generation will be the last light bulb,
To cross over to another sector an assessment is imposed,
Children are restructured from families to the state,
For implants, science must modify thoughts,
Job choices will be assigned doctrine,
Distractions are a good target to think about obeying,
Pursue the intruder to display movement control,
Dark lines smile as vampires feed,
The spy ladder grows ever narrower,
Between border bars forgotten miseries are crossed,
The Trojan horse returns to the battle of confusionisms,
The house of cards holds the pyramid of the mighty,
Defying the law leads the leader to tremble in the tower,
The engineering code decides the destinations with strategies,
Social acts are controlled with guardian slaves,
Identity is conspired to be possessed in empires,
The society of producers is the hidden structure,
Identity seeks equality by damaging measures of integration,
Utopia aspires to change morals with technical science,
A world of fiction is born feigning happiness,
New branches are integrated into the chains of rhythm,
Genetic engineering separates reproductive capacity,
Ecstasy substances plunge minds into happiness,
Weapons are exchanged for gases to put the tyrant to sleep,
The world seems happy in constant schizophrenia,
Discipline regulates with measures of dictator schemes,
A lion sleeps in the heart of every brave man,
Few see what they are but many see what they appear to be.

43 Split and You Will Win

From the UN there is a Trojan horse with tyranny,
Fascists are a located front for hierarchies,
Where dictators collect world taxes,
The identical game plan is the same original sin,
The masses conquered by the cross and hell,
Fear between hope is a priestess prison motto,
The imposition of punishment is a feeling of guilt,
A calculated cold plan controls the current human,
Same face different masks but same sides
With white gloves the handshake is different,
The double cross sign attached to the Crown of jewels and flowers,
He claimed doomed to freedom and bound to loss,
The invaders fake the fight with a mirror in reflections,
Discreet monopoly designs the perfect model,
A change of identity is introduced by dictators,
The fantasy of the past continues in the myth of the future,
Success becomes virtual to continue being marginalized,
Schools are to adapt the human to factories,
The existence of reality is creation to survive,
The love towards the neighbor is forgotten by ideas to losses,
Choosing becomes a language of seeing need,
The dictatorship of pleasure turns learning into weariness,
The crisis leads to probabilities in insecurities,
The end of privacy disturbs the illusion of consciousness,
Inflation is generated for the power of other systems,
The old rules are repeated like daily bread,
Thoughts giving answers without logic to terms,
Identity becomes a rigid block limited to choosing,
The great filter reaches cosmic Solitude for extinction.

44 Problem and Solution

Contraband circles surround the round table,
In the storm and the calm lies ecstasy
Banking vehicles are the best wash for mafias,
Anti-conflict campaigns are the hidden roots,
Losing the origin of the target is the perfect structure,
The golden triangle wraps bodies killed in traffic,
Plastered shipments are distribution without prohibition,
Tracking is dodged to not channel the target,
A good transition period is the problem with a solution,
To prevent reversion, education must be controlled,
Between crises separate the population is the moderate formula,
Cities to create uncivilized civilizations,
The big blackout is the mess to rearrange,
The tax limit will be non-inhabitant residents,
To remain but not to belong is the key to justice,
Authoritarian roots steal public opinion,
Inequality separates looking for the most effective way,
The expression of logic and dignity is not important,
The predator designs a map of the most efficient human,
Isolated bubbles obsessively seek facets,
Natural bonds leave the key in technology,
Only governed by science and the reason of control,
A brave new world has fallen asleep in cybernetic laws,
The tension of power continues on the same stage,
The holocaust is hanging on a new thread,
Forgiveness and revenge have a hole card,
The secret challenges are in kidnapping storms,
An ice will bring the deluge of the collapsed apocalypse,
The witches of hell will be the owners of heaven.

45 Rule The World

The owl behind the shadow of the domain carries the signal,
The rites of order hide in faithful devotion,
Food with adoration leaves key symbols,
An occultism that must offer satanic offerings,
The traces of scars will never be seen,
There are inconspicuous plantations with few seeds,
Reigns watch for a submissive population,
The roots are aligned to belong to the same card,
The big bad wolf hides among the sheep of the flock,
Sharp fangs just show the rules
In fearful looks only silences hide,
By educating society the path makes the change,
Some fixed squares are painted in only two colors,
A step is different to confuse with colors,
Glitter entertainment misses targets,
With distractions in trouble comes worry,
The search for the external sky sterilizes the minds,
Norms change face in fearful situations,
Explanations are peaceful to calm fears,
The round table is shielded from the outside by onlookers,
There's a tanker pointing at suspicious movements,
The movements are precise in cases of turbulence,
Meetings are elegant, experiences are required,
The process is thorough in a metallic chess,
The public face obeys the directive of the high command,
Some sinister spheres will be cleaned in words,
Some columns narrow to choose passengers,
Between thirst and hunger the knees grow weak,
The separation reduces with the tension they are scared.

46 House of Cards

Between one and the other the songs have different rhythms,
The reaction of slave strategies direct the game,
Prejudice observes where actions change,
The cell is stunned where they wrap furious,
The victims throw stones when they see progress from sides,
Being something wraps beliefs in blind pride,
Being someone is forgotten to walk blind in combat,
The game of possessing is the separation between humans,
The image is wrapped with a smile and sadness,
On stage actors take the film seriously,
The game is in colors but the player does not observe them,
The fun can be shared by not judging roles,
A dose of fear is injected into the turbulent lamb,
A pale shadow sets the line of the herd in order,
The small empire dictates the version of its truth,
Undemanding observers leave crowds powerless,
Vision is the effect of each collective movement,
When delivering the power the wings in the flight stagger,
Identity becomes a bat by not supporting itself,
Fights gather words just to distract enemies,
Between star smiles some rays can pass,
The difference is a utopia between cracked streets,
Separated sides become thieves,
The looks are hidden with differences that stun,
The ears become deaf to the trembling of what is foreign,
Mouths open expressions with false emotions,
Between problems and solutions is based punishment,
The untrained mind believes all circumstances,
By training the consciousness the castle will become stable.

47   Between The Debt and The Sword

Leonese roar between bars without emotional cries,
The solution reaction are the best alternatives,
Narrow discord is the key to separate branches,
Introducing the United Nations is the perfect control plan,
Fooling public thought is effective on needs,
The steps of support leave sequels undetected,
Running the economy is a virus for horrible poverty,
Butchers are spied on to follow defeats,
To introduce world authority is to continue causing conflicts,
The focus on international discord is a political play,
The main branches are branch protection,
Advancing medicine includes reliance on microchips,
Members are the global elite organizing the agenda,
Money from nothing marginalizes the life of the indebted,
A constant knot causes economic cycles to steal,
NATO treaties claim to be free trade but in secret,
The order agenda injects the law into divided zones,
Restrictions rob independence of thought,
Training with dictatorships becomes a prison,
In seven columns write the restrictions without exits,
Virtual reality obscures the door that is open,
The name of the law destroys proofs of rights,
The villainous heroes know the secret exits,
Sorcerers fight to survive instead of living,
The moral compass is left with sequels and appears civilized,
Where evil disobeys god and persecutes the government,
Heaven ceases to be a magical place for something prosperous,
The horizon of progress becomes deviant society,
Evil humanity becomes its own judge.

48 The Clavicle of Solomon

In the ark of the covenant the third mighty king of Israel.
Surrounded with sublime riches and noble wisdom,
Mystical language interprets in the nature of forests,
Doors open between crystals with alchemy of powers,
Between spells and talismans magical formulas appear,
The key to the secret book becomes infinity,
The occultism of times carries mysteries of gods,
Sublime content silences powerful spells,
Texts invoke the eternal for control and obedience,
Angels and demons are marked as guides,
Finding enigmatic signs in lost conspiracy,
Heaven descends to earth where divine intrigue lies,
A serpent peeks out at diabolical sacrifices,
A virtuous angel casts lightning knowledge,
Roots branch out in the glistening darkness,
Rabbis keep holy scriptures in bronze,
A ring engraved seal with Jewish traditions,
The star pentagram is silent dominance,
The colorless pillars mark spiritual symbols,
Protection is designed over the gates of evil,
The world meets the physical in the invisible,
An Acacia table is covered in pure gold in harmony,
Between past and future a candlestick rules,
Seven arms lead to the inner challenge system,
Rituals with twelve tribes in the mountains are consecrated,
Where the ark of the covenant keeps the commandments,
The chest holds the boards with the rodand the stone,
The connection forms the pact and sits among the clouds,
The temple of Jerusalem receives the cults rendered.

49 The Eternal Worker

One more brick becomes a shadow of mud,
Inequality is a food farm in control,
The biological and technological is the division formula,
Visualization will be a disintegrated synthetic force,
The integrated disorder is infiltrated in few feelings,
To overwhelm disobedience using few thoughts
The contract of dishonor will trap robotic humans,
Kindness will be to dishonor the peace of the sleeping slave,
The face of the same coin is the illusion of a double,
The effect of the link follows behind the hidden veil,
They seek the protection of the powerful for insecure dreams,
In slave piety hides artillery of control,
Human farms created for sinister purposes,
Sentinels watch the movements of guards,
Steps sink into mud so as not to see their footprints,
The adventure loses strength drums sound without ideas,
A sunken grave chained by governments,
The glances are narrow in silences that oppress,
Campaigns raise flights but the storm persists,
The knees bend to dine without regrets,
At every corner doors close as they sigh,
A look back puts debts with massive blockades,
The vultures flow with false speculations,
Uncontrolled investors restrict human rights,
A blackout of hope turns to sad sounds,
The custom daydreams to feel the calm day,
Swimming in cold seas, destinations are fed,
They hit bottom without complaining to come out towards the shore,
Fatigue to the goal collects the crumbs of progress,
The looks of the black sea remain in divided cracks.

50 Conditional Freedom

The balloon of Alcatraz I entered walls in the centuries,
The words are heard as mental liberation,
The sheepdog's scary voice rushes the line,
Delivering power and chasing the extraordinary strange,
The strategic base has time in the formation,
The formula of the times is strengthened with appearance,
The fiber is strengthened well rushed to the root,
Thought is doubt as senseless reason,
The puppet strings seem safe in the face of obstacles,
The mind appears to be close to the body without feeling,
The designer updates the documents regularly,
The lazy mind ignores the conditions of sentence,
The flight is observed but it does not rise to its destination,
The sky is clear but a smell is perceived burnt,
A generation program is well established,
The following passengers board without looking back,
One timed effect helps follow the next,
Rights are not hidden, they already reflect conditions,
The engine of evolution only with silence asks,
A black cross is seen on human faces,
They look at each other in surprise with a marked scar,
Everyone wearing the mask just changes colors
The eyes are only days with nuances of sentences,
Between corners they cross but nobody recognizes each other,
Customs repeat themselves by ignoring conditions,
A new vehicle waits without answers to the past,
Paradise is free between beliefs that drag,
The sea keeps waves, the sailor steers the ship,
The unlimited passenger chooses the reins of control.

51 Behind Bars

Shock troops and psychiatrists grafting psychoses,
Modifications are discreet by changing behaviors,
Submission is the goal within the corrupt order,
The secret enemy raises black magic in rituals,
War keeps the antidote destroying morale,
The invasion of nations speaks in credible ignorance,
The hungry valley with the demons of the world,
Weak sloths clinging to the crystal ball,
Consulting in the empty music of credulous illusion,
Celebrating the undesirable to share gossip,
Empty states of life applauded by screenfame,
The door to the temple of fools forms slave groups,
Infinite matter with attention grows to exist,
A sound of drums will cover signs in poison,
Intraterrestrial combats appear from mountains,
The caves seem to be free behind invisible bars,
The river of the human farm has no solid bridges,
Temporary relief only calms the desert storm,
Where poisoned roses are injected into poor children,
The cape shakes the wind in the operation musketeer,
The quicksand clock is on its last beats
The mystery of the beast implants hate to divide,
The flashes discharge the crystals in lightning bolts,
Thought control casts out the fire within,
Letting go of feelings in a vicious circle,
The volcanoes will turn oceans into vapor of sighs,
Violent kingdoms snatch patient hopes,
In the thousandth year after the thousandth year death begins,
Ownership becomes orders not to choose.

52 Swim in The World

Before the unseen a visible throne had been lost,
The best slave is the one who thinks he is free and does not fight,
The heat of anger can be swallowed by grasshoppers,
As we enter the cosmic age, new seas open,
A hermetic power preserves roots of wisdom,
A cliff blindly dragged a path of believers,
The key to wisdom is in the power of the mind,
The pendulum of rhythm is in evolution transmuting,
The law of individualization is the meeting of the cosmos,
A bohemian night of butterflies perfumes the air,
Streams of clover blaze sweet fragrances,
Between colored bells with the freshness of dawn,
Some melodies flame with ecstasy in heavenly glories,
Years of mistakes and successes are powerful tools,
Make the enemy a friend preach those of control,
A whirlwind clinging to the crystal ball in beliefs,
The sentinels of heaven leave recorded origins,
A spiral touches the limit to find descent,
The collective mind lives in the same mission for years,
The servants of the system are for blind obedience,
Learning in unlearning awakens the linear path,
Living without limits is interconnected at a universal level,
Immortal pioneers without return will conquer Mars,
There is no going back in the field of perfect storm,
Natural resources are unlimited due to pollution,
The futuristic world becomes avatar to survive,
The game of power no longer has a King with a golden throne,
Destructive morality must be tied to the lost spirit,
The principles of power are the judgments of contributing.

53 Web Maze

Someone dances between melodies of other generations,
In dangerous waters there are uncontrollable nuclear forces,
A storm blows on a scale of aristocracy,
The blind journalists write what they obey,
The crystal ball recalls the cults of the mafia,
The destructive system wraps the economy in poverty,
The empire affects the human mind in submissive conditions,
Education a magic circle with guided fantasies,
The techniques are simulation games for isolations,
Behavior modification influences thoughts,
Change agents identify those who resist,
Where the catalyst continues to control the system,
Serving the collective is the goal for dialectical materialism,
The conflict of opposite poles is in the same philosophy,
Liberty is designed to obey the government,
Critical thinking turns into bullying and punishment,
Health submits to the society of observant desire,
The cancer of the privileged sits in the labyrinth,
An iceberg plants doubts that scatter into the ocean,
Waves arrive as an entity where sharks attack,
Clever freedom faces the game room,
Among many shouts and jeers, the entertained applaud,
Masks with whims go towards a phantom torrent,
Darkness awaits the believer with a cataract void,
A great hurricane swallowing wasted debris,
The dormant crystal generation is carried to loads,
Fashion dresses in reason implanted in networks,
The contradiction becomes with the war of feelings,
Playgrounds hang on the web of strategies.

54 Missing

Some darts are thrown while infants disappear,
The demand rule is constant under a full moon,
The hidden caves are never sated before kidnappings,
The praise of power with exchanges are just facades,
Level 33 will follow the espionage of the control thoroughly,
The songs of Nazis are very illustrious in the lineages,
Secret nets from underground carry the currents,
The hermetic cross is the force of the reptilian food,
The great council erases old era for secret revolution,
The secret files control the supply of oxygen,
Medieval transparency guards fearful scandals,
The enigmas of the Vatican are sad dark nights,
The city engulfs people on the way back from ground zero,
The battlefield is an ancient disease,
The supreme bosses impose new hierarchies,
The ark of the covenant signs monarchisms in pacts,
The chained servants of power submit,
The strings move in the shadow of governments,
The fall of rebirth leaves lodges in silent rituals,
The deluge drowns tense stories in lost steps,
Seeds of the new order have been sown for centuries,
With humor they calm discord between doses of glances,
The masks in spells are solemnly protected,
The tradition of rituals carries penalties for betrayal,
The pendulum moves carefully in a horizontal line,
The vertical tide tends to change the currents,
The sword of mystery is trained in the temples,
Honorary Degrees Risk Freemasons Values,
The square of the compass in the sacred marks the rhythm.

55 Hermetic Tradition

White gloves serene the hidden traces,
Hanging chandeliers blaze in color,
Initiation ceremonies in signal recognition
Between the outer temple lies an inner temple,
The universal energy where the sun rises in the east,
The brotherhood of the moon darkens the offerings,
The compass in challenges is the tool for construction,
Between rectitude and balance the formula incubates levels,
The rope around the neck forms the mark of the umbilical cord,
The Star King connects his chain to the powerful earth,
On the path of life there is a body of a feline sphinx,
The figure of a woman advances through the raging water,
A pacifist ship faces not seeing the light of the lighthouse,
A shipwreck against the rocks is caused by submerging,
The reversible order is respected with rules and sentences,
The chessboard in duality defines the future,
Passwords in words with the directing hands,
The high trajectory with the degrees progresses on ridges,
The union in symbology raises the dome of the movement,
The teaching in the dogmas is transmitted in silence,
The insignia of the great Sarmiento sealed with the dragon,
The star illuminates the entrance with the forged signs,
The sacred law trains apprentices with the aim of supporting,
Narcissistic societies are taught to create the system,
The brotherhood of mystery seeks to form defenders,
The main principles are scattered throughout the world,
Oaths and rites squeeze the hand in privilege,
Lodges of veterans drag their spirit in transformation,
The smiles of the pendulum separate time into principles.

Baton obedience programs the dark generation,
With manipulation the imaginable behavior is modified,
Hierarchy worship selects bloodlines of fear,
Dependent linked with steps to follow members,
Bombardment of love and misfortune is the cage of zombies,
Hidden sleepers feel their dead eyes,
Culture of being protected as grasshoppers chases,
Some fun goes by soothing timers
The constraint rules are fixed on the keys,
Learning classes are obligation to remember,
When picking up the certificate, the look has another owner,
The movements to changes weigh as chained,
Junk content is crossed as arrow,
The Pokémon of the turn reinforces the implanted beliefs,
Reigns with unattainable stairs are observed,
The mind adapts not to think for fear of fatigue,
Illusions sink with easy workouts,
The voice becomes silent, the ears almost deaf,
The eyes do not see far for fear of losing the cage,
The questions have no answers as there are programs,
The structure is run by hypnotizing fun,
Families are enemies by standing in the way of silence,
Opinions are daggers by interfering in contradiction,
The pillars already have a content with strategies,
Values are empty and trained with obedience,
There are tears in corners but feelings do not exist
A black hole hides silent time bombs,
A slow fire is destroying the invisible lives,
The clouds travel without borders to show their Freedom.

57 Hidden Challenges

The submerged valley expands with hybrid lineages,
The genetic codes must follow the empire,
The Cruze of tribes is separated by breed of cattle,
Population control by secret means is sterilized,
The means of restrictions are scientific development,
There are innocent explanations rewarded by the elite,
New order models must involve eugenics,
The green army movement manipulated for interests,
Gray waves and fossils in their tones are camouflaged,
Fuel systems have no free limits,
The wand of decisions has a serious protocol,
Civil war engineering is targeted for depopulation,
The sterilized methods are implanted in water and food,
The structure for power with challenges flourishes,
Myths keep silent thinkers without opinion,
Eclipses will mark sudden winter changes,
The fourth lap will go into geological convulsion,
Sharks on shores approach with the apocalypse
Confidence is dangerous by ignoring instinctual issues,
The gloomy sun abandons those who abandon the earth,
On the dark plains the cold penetrates the roots,
The black magician is selected for the desired mission,
The extremes are used for infiltrated changes,
The children of the matrix wait to choose the pill,
The predator made the prisoners docile like insects,
The masses watch themselves between hidden challenges,
The permanent servants carry out command orders,
A bush hides the invisible rules steps.

58 Sleeping Cops

It's no longer important to be how intriguing it is to seem,
The label is the image with sound of powers,
Protest marches are like photo gatherings,
The vigilantes walk with uniform and without brain,
Privileged appearances appear to give shine to footwear,
The enemy of good traps his mind in false truths,
Identity oppresses reason in slave medals,
The rejection becomes a crime in case any tribe interferes,
Lines are carefully followed to accuse terrorists,
The levels are taboo between prohibition to questions,
The union that appeases is to repeat what is imposed,
False morality willing to save the world in ideologies,
The leader becomes the favorite fable with a star smile,
Bad and good people are divided to play along,
The stories of the winner are first evaluated,
Offensive theories become delinquency,
Those who shout in public out of delirium are imprisoned,
The looks with doubts are the enemy that spies,
The poor poorly dressed man is pushed into the dark corner,
The one who laughs very loud is a madman for the madhouse,
He who does not believe in vaccines is a virus for the population,
Interpretive spaces are cracks to watch,
Ideas can change but with the same method,
Colors can be observed without moving their position,
Racism is punished but with a hidden face it is kicked,
Women are protected to subjugate men,
Thefts are reported but the cameras are off,
Compliant uniforms for the watchtower method,
Blind winners of the new holy scriptures.

59   Cold Eyes

Feelings do not exist between the five corners,
From deep caves there are quotes of secrets,
The exchanges of pacts kneel feelings,
In the atrocity of smiles fearful calls sound,
Eager sharp claws devour human bodies,
Innocent souls fall into cold and cruel hands,
The underground caverns eagerly await blood,
Dark celebrations sponsor the foundations,
The darkness appears asleep to the hidden interior,
The old testament drags hypocrisy from antiquity,
Feeling guilt is the perfect pill to seek forgiveness,
Acclaiming the fire helps is to continue burning at the stake,
Seeking justice without justifying is a chained sin,
The old speeches never let the good triumph,
Recognizing cruelty is never enough in coldness,
Guilty bridges of the past open guillotines to the future,
Pointing and punishing hides the traces of the accuser,
Weapons expand to radicalize borders,
Technology leads to religions full of obstacles,
Salvation disguises attract minds lost in doubt,
The school exam is dominating with grades,
The powerful faces implanted the title that separates,
Ladder of measures for military purposes without real territory,
Society of tiredness programmed for effectiveness,
Accelerated patience is contemplated productivity,
The human quality is brief for separate connections,
The implantation of fast life altering values,
Covers mold minds to be designs and contents,
Instincts with distracted differences lose their destiny.

60 Handprints

Trips in chrome tubes in thousandths of a second,
A dark bonfire reflects faces without any identity,
A shiver runs through the epochs of the sleeping desert,
The moral compass claims to be imaginable and civilized,
Swapping demonic sickness for mental,
Pointing out good and evil, chains are engraved on the horizon,
The poor man praises interest because he collects from his product,
Mortality risks subtly sound offshoring,
Exploitation does not change the direction of the millennium,
The moral ethical fixation drags the accomplices to silence,
The members of fiscal entities advance with moderation,
The concept of good embraces the cracks with that of evil,
The global in the cosmic attracts mutual destruction,
When the light pierced the darkness, solidarity is born,
Wandering in the void awaits the compass of independence,
Following profiles but not identity is mechanical perfection,
There are punishers. observed without spaces to have errors,
The stock market dehumanized by objectives,
The reign of fear and terror lurks around every corner,
The fictional tribe is indistinguishable from the real show,
A hole of old still believes in Santa Clause,
Small conquests lead to a great course,
Life does not ask, it only arrives and makes its answers,
A little monster grows where good meets evil,
In the footprints there are united writings to read in the Palm,
Arrogance and goodness meet without limits or borders,
The night of time enters the cage of the present,
Changing responses is evolution.
Changing the question is revolution.

61 Persecuted Life

The empires of the future are mind controls,
The sun rises life is a blessing but in competition
Strength comes from an indomitable will,
Physical courage raises the consent that silences,
By denying the system a drum sounds to another rhythm,
Power derives from consent to the chosen dance,
Cowardice asks questions before opponents who oppress,
There are disposable and fanciful consuming minds,
It is the invasion of fools where fakers are respected,
Fanciful combinations with rigged elections,
The villain is ignored so that the work continues in intrigue,
The theory is rewritten with a fictional demand,
The work forms the perfect simulacrum of persecution,
Cyberpunk viewers closer to the actors,
The new era of false morality gobbles up for sleepwalking,
Madness is repeating the same thing hoping that something will change,
The digital cosmos freezing reality in a black box,
Science and technology drives the formula for disasters,
The scientific society sounds like the new priests,
Criticism snowballs to isolate,
Humanity between surprises embraces the giant leader,
The cave monster sends a poem of caresses
addicted entertainment is a beginning without end,
A moral temple created its own recognition rival,
Realizing that you are the lion and not the sheep, you wake up,
The mirror of the inner circle is the key to progress,
A bubble breaks between waves of real colors,
The key to Freedom is union with nature,
A drop of water is enough to protect a start.

62   The Whole and Nothing

You can run but you can't escape the after,
You avert your eyes from time between confused smiles,
A bad smell is felt between its footprints, it traps us,
Starting over restores the traces of what has been lived,
The individual trap tends to many and no commitment,
The solutions are visible labels but without guarantee,
Dictators of pleasure far removed from reality,
Society of prisoners with simulacra of their own satisfaction,
An unemployment patch covers a glass floor,
The freedom is created as a photographic exhibition,
The simulation made fictional substituting abilities,
Trapped in lives accommodated by recycling cages,
Submitted to the theater of being observed and special,
The sacred desecrated by brand popularity,
Searching for oneself has already lost reality in unreality,
The spectacle of the original is devoured by the image,
Without moderation the festival of consumption is cultivated,
The symbol of the three arrows engulfs the third world,
Contamination circles from victim to victimizer,
With miserable shortcuts all corners are touched,
Wealth vigilantes manipulate schizophrenic triumphs,
Ignorance becomes a myth to continuewith inflation,
The so-called privileged look at others coldly,
fear of emptiness, they seek rules in satisfaction,
Speeches in marginalized moral convictions from poor,
An endless chain spinning in addicted arguments,
Poor and rich always disunited on the side of the equation,
All with a path to salvation in a wild parting,
A sea of explanations in sacrifices that oppress.

63   Injection of Ideas

Life of saints injected with the softness of delirium,
Sinless evangelists under robes of silent screams,
Cracks bleed hidden waiting to be found
A golden space is still at the top with goals,
The occultist of wealth from the pyramid directs,
Russian roulette is a quick scenario to be invisible,
The levels follow the rules of nefarious exploitation,
Unreality feels rich like a Tower of Babel,
The existential explodes in a call of infinite ascent,
Looking down something close to oblivion seems terrifying,
Something distantly known disguises itself in unknown traces,
Looking for paradise, the present moment is forgotten,
The cults are worshiped but the ends far apart,
Between changing nations the lapses follow powers,
Barriers lose stability in cultures without limits,
The land of Nederland in time acceleration,
Social life devoured by the experience of the spectacle,
The combat of appearance is the primordial content,
The future of identity turning the world into pleasure,
Infantilized society bombarded by sensations,
The immediate takes the power to feel adoration,
Intensive programs for children without giving them space to play,
Self-satisfaction is unable to face risk,
The imposed work is an ideal for hypnotic victimhood,
The victim role is the continuing key to injecting ideas,
The subjugated are the good savages of the conquerors,
The oppressed stripped of identity look for guilty,
Without values in education they create separate peoples,
Maturity demands acceptance, understanding and commitment.

64 Obey!!

Harmless slaves create their own identity,
Selling themselves as meek they are conquered by leaders,
The oppressed end up dreaming their Freedom with ideas,
Faced with fear they praise the gods they reject,
The outcasts submit by showing themselves without ambition,
Thinkers with unfortunate feelings fall,
The greatest power is knowing how to agree with the devil's dialogue,
The answer of what they want to hear attracts puppets,
Control begins with the necessary for the unnecessary,
Mutual observers willing to punish each other in criticism,
Noisy fever lights torches in mistrust,
The monster devours the hungry supporting demonstrations,
The groups polarize by enclosing themselves in bubbles,
Angry watchers within fear with challenges to the future,
An unlimited desire is the craving that is never achieved,
Outbursts appear with a supportive dark side
To modify behavior you need culture war,
The juggling attraction for social street vendors,
Engineering filters imposing cybernetic theory,
Ideologies remain sequestered in eternal presents,
The empires of the future will be the empires of the mind,
The mask of warriors trained in storytellers,
The supreme revelation haunts the marked programs,
The tradition of authorities forms the slave fair,
Domination marks the stamp on the obedient structure,
The nests of tradition never go out to the open sea,
Chains lead to the abyss of bitter subjection,
Greed organizes and will be disoriented democracy,
The children of history seek to arrive before but without objective.

65 Reptile Blood

The serpent gods searching for the garden of eden,
Golden apples remember eternity,
A dragon leaves some fearsome stories with conditions,
Some symbols of temptations with evil looks,
A garden with appearances marks forbidden forms,
Some ancient trees bear bonds of events,
Subterranean lizards among the dance of snakes,
There is a gigantic chamber with crossbreeding programs,
Among malevolent rituals the invaders live hidden,
Secret societies experiment with human DNA,
Network of agent infiltrators united in brotherhood,
Between the veins of the grand canyon a sanctuary hides,
One wavelength is introduced as paranormal,
The core of the parable is to distract with scenes,
The reptilian brain is expression among complete crusaders,
Where Hollywood movies mold the human mind,
Like a chameleon changes colors from the burrow,
Reptilian abilities bind control with torrents,
The perfect structure is appearance of holographs,
The truth is incomprehensible even in forms of evidence,
A programming device advances in dimensions,
The shadow of encounters is distinguished by blood,
Between levels of races separate humans for experiments,
Some tests disappear due to errors in the process,
Intruding opponents are guarded with weapons,
Public silences are imposed before hidden roots,
Pacts are closed between the elect of the system,
Failures in restrictions have death sentences.

66 The Basis of The System

The symbols relate hearing and vision in lineages,
The reins of generations are delivered by brotherhood,
The baton must tune with the key,
The race is broadcast with evaluation tests,
Vibrational veils reside in the emotional psyche,
Reptilian draconians fueled by emotional energy,
Calling science and creating a new society,
A level impact is conditioned for robotics,
On the brink of Armageddon depopulation unfolds,
A well-coordinated apocalypse for the chosen ones,
Plans turn their backs for complimentary privacy,
Freedom has counted the hours before being subdued,
Consumer demand will be delayed due to shortages,
The chains are lining up for a new course of history,
The bubble expands where the army enslaves,
The Sunday movement is advancing in the dark,
Armageddon invades with diseases without cure,
The nuclear force in contamination arrives in a moment,
Landless citizens in dead-end wars,
Science understands freedom that is equal to inclination,
The biological desires are changed into order paper,
The definition becomes implants under bars,
Human happiness in the hands of political chimera,
The triumph achieved is anonymous in the eyes of the people,
Causes pass between survivors waiting for opportunities,
Getting up and starting over is the light of the next day,
As long as the causes remain unavoidable, life goes away.

67 Looking for Beauty

The impoverished adult child adapts his gaze to what is childish,
Learn to teach from the brain of the learner,
A genius is the story of a failure for being curious,
With sacrifice the passion obtains the success of the effort,
To create is to learn to imagine from the one who learns,
To be born is to adapt the adult gaze to the childish gaze,
To be silent to listen has silences that conquer the voice,
The happiness of a project lives in curiosity,
Courage supported from trust is rebirth,
With virtues and defects, each explosive is a dogma,
Moments of attention are divine gifts,
Living with each other is an art in constant testing,
The jungle city is a complex society with infinite challenges,
Bringing out the inner ethics is to visualize an excellent melody,
A smile to the painter creates the harmony of the image,
Being important is being different leaving traces in appreciation,
Children are the teachers for the development of greatness,
Awakening strength in courage is inspiration of instinct,
In each small project the scenario of a genius grows,
Path is to awaken the heart to find greatness,
Uncertainty is like a fan to hold,
The course of the miracle has united hell and paradise,
Traveling light builds the great adventure of life,
The minutes slip away with no options to be bought,
Fighting for orientation is content that elevates,
In consciousness is the recipe for undefeated water,
With any number of defects, the basis is not to cultivate hatred,
The garden blooms in the blind because love is magic
Beauty is a hive where honey is natural.

68 The Hidden Look

The capacity of the potential returns to submerge,
Great cities under tunnels in the surface of poplars,
Beings among insignia of the blue triangle with the dragon,
The cold-blooded hierarchy are the base of the vehicle,
Since wars, human sacrifice is the main link,
Rituals with adrenaline are demanded by castes,
Rows after immense areas of transformed hybrids,
Several horrified levels seven for experiments,
Genetic crossings double looks with macabre scenes,
You mix half human and animal creatures in desolation,
Screams from massacres to be frozen in reserves,
Warehouses of embryos in stages of development,
Scientific refrigerators for implants from vaccines,
Between crosses of chameleons is the hall of nightmares,
Human slave children working for the reptiles,
Rapidly built tunnels for advanced technology,
Underground nuclear-powered machines melt walls,
Control origins linked from the planet Mars,
Secret test bases with vast caverns,
Fallen angels with wings are the race of bird-men,
The royalty of powers with scales and cold blood,
Without emotions or feelings they absorb the energies,
Insiders seize the psyche for power,
Between genocide of wars something abstract distracts him,
Reproduction programs the dark history is lineage,
The occult look of alien resurrection is yet to come,
The Sumerians of Mesopotamia portray their gods,
Traces of reproductions have been imposed for centuries.

69 The Peak of The Challenge

The iguana and the chameleon in resonance of changes,
The halls of mirrors are the perfect distraction,
The men in black act to promote programs,
Between appearances some trips are hallucinations,
Some apparitions in dimensional planes operate,
Abductions for mental abductions as hybrids,
It is an important link secrets of shuttle tubes,
The blue pyramid marks circles for lineages of control,
The Phoenix bird is the symbol of the selected brotherhood,
The compass of the masons between coffins hides,
Sealed tablets with open sharp smiles,
Majestic houses built by the network of brotherhood,
An iron fist bends in caged generations,
The dark shadow becomes private industry,
A quiet conquest towards very busy hours,
Sensitive data is observed in the imperial peak,
The imposed religion pretends to be called the social good,
The new political era remembers that the code is the law,
The impulses are reflected to make faces of astonishment,
Evidence projects have airtight chests,
The opinion window is constantly saturated,
The culprits jump ropes with clever strategies,
An angel opens its wings visiting lambs for caresses,
Defendants stop charges with tempting bets,
Civilized apes calmly respond to the abyss,
The nostalgic with fever loses strength by acceptance,
Blow the flag with denials of the tyrant,
The civil battlefield has restricted weapons,
Those in the gray suit carry a briefcase with the country of tomorrow.

70 The Elite Controls

Being always behind the shadow turns the enigmas,
The masters of the world between crowns and thirteen families,
The great reset is a rebrand,
Promotion is a digital and biological physical internet,
IOT sensors enable robotic communication,
IOT technology is RAND corporation device,
Your content will be able to collect biometric data,
The main function to observe the Health and produces changes,
Integrating devices can alter the function of the body,
By implanting IOT, no part of the HUMAN body will escape its
interference,
A fleeting strategy is to analyze the genetic material,
Not even babies can escape this nightmare,
Every bodily function is constantly monitored,
The goal is to have more control with the word freedom,
Digital pills will be information tools,
Medical compliance will be the guardian of measures,
The villains will only be cartoonists of the blind world,
The real with the fake will be promoted in the conditions,
Carbon versus silicon is in constant attack,
Embracing the artificial will be the raging anti-human agenda,
Body nanotubes are inner trackers,
The union to restore the trajectory as a species,
Affected in identity bowing before royalty,
Everything can be removed in the blink of an eye,
Authority reaching from the abyss of hell,
The world order will be appointed to life slavery,
You will own nothing and you will be happy.

71 The Oasis

The metaverse a journey climbing Mount Everest,
A place where the limits of reality are the imagination,
The union of the universe between universal pyramids,
A casino the size of a beautiful and free planet,
A hug with the avatar of the dragon friend of destiny,
Planets with lineages for imaginary empire battles,
Convertible artifacts for experiential domains,
Powerful random worlds where life is choice,
Risky items between levels of accepted risks,
Life plays in the jump with altered double control,
Between doors to the abyss a number becomes zero,
An emblem laser between balances and technologies,
Between distraction and addition there is a DNA symbol,
Virtual reality in connection with the almighty,
The beginning mage with ultimate abilities,
Wrapping the alchemy of learning with magnetism,
Intrigue draws creation to the test of ecstasy,
The rhythms change directions for mysteries with enigmas,
The bottomless pit opens, rising smoke of darkness,
The sun darkens and the air becomes nightmares,
A scorpion wrapped in angel and king is still on the throne,
A tower frees the world from the weary hermit,
There's a quick goodbye where the stars wait,
The trips of great dimensions are reflected in the artificial,
The demonic world mixes with humanity,
Quantum resources will be future dominant prophecy,
For the alarm to sound planes are not linear,
People come to the oasis for all they can do,
People stay at the oasis for all they can be.

72 The Sun in The Darkness

The grand mafia lodge among persecuted Benedicts,
Puzzle moves are exchanged with pawns,
The skull and bones society is of secret members,
The deer island closes its gates at midnight,
Blue blood follows from the opium with the slave racket,
From the great east the flag runs through the genes,
The clan of lords follows the agenda of the reproductive scheme,
The guardians of the fourth dimension include with filters,
Trapping the nations from the foundations of communism,
Structuring societies from the top down,
There is an invisible hand that controls the direction of the world,
The current of hidden and gloomy thoughts,
The league of the just a sinister game with synthesis,
Fear is the best conductor to steal energy,
The red cross the symbol of recognition in the brotherhood,
There is a massage arm for public opinions,
The stage of life arises from a collectivemind,
The tradition of founders is sustained by a protective mafia,
The saviors putting the global chain congested,
Conspiring for system events to happen,
A cloud seeding emerges with new threats,
A heavenly river provokes weather tricks,
The great atomic condemnation disguises itself as a firecracker,
The stratospheric injection is invaded by aerosols,
With colorless petals scent of smoke spreads,
Radiation mirrors have few cracks,
A discreet ribbon inside falls submerged,
The board counts the cards on the field of competitions,
The cruel angel makes decisions without certainty in the riddle.

73 Image of Coldness

A classic mosaic-style diversion trap,
Muddy waters protect circulation in double crossings,
The allies are a cold hunting team,
The designs have hidden compartments on the outside,
Image pain does not exist in feelings,
The tins cover up the solo organization,
Purposes have the condition sealed in diversions,
Obscuring the guilty is part of a central faction,
Lone assassins are supported by ravens,
Organized crime has a trance course,
Platonic corruption forgets sins and virtues,
There is coldness to learn to control mental shadows,
Dancers with private property move theirbodies,
The Fabian society disguises the secret wolf as a sheep,
Establish psychological control for submission and power,
The double standard of the top has no border limits,
Transhumanism dragging people into eco science,
Theoretical systems to serve the tyrant of laws,
Seeking immortality in robotic transcendence,
The human mind converted into a symbiotic society,
The threads are driven implanted fear for survival,
The secret fraternity ruthlessly confiscates assets,
Turn peoples into docile and unthinking hierarchies,
Shock therapy controls the essence to world progress,
The British elite plan the extinction system,
Around the corner nuclear wars await,
Behind the scenes a defensive goal becomes offensive,
Masked alliances are victims of friendly fire,
Pictures stay together cold sad stories.

74 Smile with Purpose

Five tax havens shelter the corruption of defaults,
Territories destined for the diversion of criminal offenses,
Knots of rope climb the cracks in heritage,
Neoliberalism is homicidal and also suicidal,
A world ship without doors sails as it pleases,
A forbidden forest hides a furious monster,
From ancient Egypt heralding birth of order,
The manipulative paradise manipulating the blindest,
Lodge of alliances with the symbols of seals demanded,
Each lower level does not know the objective of the higher level,
The stamp foundation always justified for freedom,
Master plans programmed for the people to program,
The thought lost among advanced orchestras,
Hellfire Club Secret Society,
Physical reality transforms the brotherhood into lodges,
Subtly replaced monarchs for democracy,
From a conjured dome child trafficking hides,
Where the heart is torn with the broken soul,
Cover-ups of stocks with corruption processes,
Kidnapped children to sell to the rich and famous,
Sinister characters from the shadow without feelings,
City of children with dark destructive destinations,
Luxury houses with scandalous blackmail for silences,
Appearances of jokes leaves defenseless victims,
Between hidden crimes justice becomes impossible,
The investigations are closed with the media,
Documents are destroyed where abuses are buried,
The persecutions oppress with codes of silence,
Convictions for telling the truth enslave and threaten,
Covering the traces between consumed addictions.

75 Awakening from The Nightmare

A masterstroke cunningly approaches the target,
Breaking the spiral of despair opens doors,
Life continues in continuous lines from acts,
The worst cages are fears and created appearances,
The world elite is the creation of the collective field,
Liberation is in the activation of the infinite mind,
The eternal experiences the physical world through thought,
Every environment is generated by visited energies,
The attraction are layers that are attracted by magnetism,
The veil in tears is the effect of the daily struggle,
The gods of fire and brimstone snatch paradise,
The mirrors reflect the landscape patterns created,
The seven upper and lower planes are levels,
The creation contains sealed diplomatic bags,
The extraterrestrial gods is a college of stories,
The invisible lord creates closed and separate minds,
The unnoticed enemy is the people themselves without control,
Uniting nations among enemies is a dangerous weapon,
Unnoticed we enter the sunset of life,
The house of hope is in the heart,
The projects of the mind are visualized physically,
The giant gods leave potential in vibratory spheres,
A seat in the dark blocks the exit in the box,
A tracking team disembarks with interference,
The children of the earth are also of the stars,
From other areas of the galaxy there is an antiquity,
The shining ones form the image of creation,
The hall of mirrors lifts the veil of truth,
The land of free is the same facade if there is a spider web.

The Name of The Wind

Manipulation is creation of collective acceptance,
The reflection of reality is by adding bullets to the cannon,
Each frequency is the same space in waves,
The wheel of light passes levels of harmonies in feelings,
Thoughts are transmissions of magnetic layers,
Interferences collide by vibrating in different dimensions,
The shell is a female symbol, instinctive creative force,
Consciousness is a whole team sharing solutions,
The genetic lab leaves sunken clues of encounters,
Wars are a banquet of energy for jailers,
The victim mentality creates the reality of it,
Fear and guilt suppress self-esteem for protection,
Stories and ceremonies are origin from the same source,
The current of corruptions is an asteroid belt,
The religions of today are the recycling of ancient stories,
Symbolic prison figures are lost in avalanches,
The mystery schools are culmination of races,
The mental prison is manipulation and control of the mass,
A philosophical doctrine is concealed inconfidence,
The dragon line meridians maintain their lineage,
The guardians are generated and feed on negative energy,
Designs in inequality is the doctrine of infinite potential,
In the great world simulation chaos will stop man,
A tense world will be the beginning of the end without knowing,
Between despair and anger, hate breaks pillars,
The prison consciousness is endowed with fire,
So that everyone serves but does not dominate the system,
A long and bitter battle catches the conflicts,
Solomon's temple is stellar for constellations.

77 World Fourth Generation

A parallel way towards the same level of the target,
The universal soldier giving away his body to the leaders,
An eternal return is in the mounts of the elite,
The fantasies of speeches are the desires of peoples,
Word echoes run behind the scenes,
Folk tales are easy prey for manipulation,
The game material continues to include the full plan,
Public opinion is only speeches of a facade,
The old goddess of democracy routine is old agenda,
The delicate diplomacy are contents of montages,
Poisons to compete destroy temples,
Light and darkness turn reflections into metamorphosis,
The ghost of social justice dies muttering,
Covering the pain with oblivion nightmares lengthen,
Some loose leaves blow in old lost winds,
Religion buries itself where science takes hold,
From balconies cries of shadows are heard cloudy,
The men of the world leave ashes in chimneys,
Giant archangels reflect the human spirit,
Spouting spells that invade the lost infinity,
Defeated restlessness hails kindness to the stars,
The misery of fear bristles the skin of tired age,
Dust covers the image of the adapted passerby,
The past noon is cut on the shores of the sea,
An enigma between trees observes the centuries of the forest,
Delusions are drawn between breezes of cold eclipses,
A bolt of lightning opened the window with a destiny pursued,
Looking back, he comes out of jail but not from the sentence,
The garden must be cleaned before it can be watered again.

78 Life of Dreams

The continuation of dreams is a talisman of the spirit,
A kind of skeleton that you must add the meat,
There is a treasure in the sea to plunge into divinity,
Taking a leap in the dark a garden appears,
There is a treasure of pearls for eternal children,
A beautiful hug turns into a sweet stream,
A link becomes a ritual of transition,
The levels of the energetic is the root continuum,
The atmosphere is in the environment of the observed landscape,
When the cement breaks a beautiful flower is born,
Someone behind is on their knees in the rubble,
A letter burns in the fire but is not consumed,
The current of the fountain moved to the hidden mystery,
It is the hero's journey to understand destiny,
Diving into silence you hear the inner voice,
Create what we dream creates the heavenly on earth,
The hidden divine search with the esoteric of witchcraft,
The tarot united with the roots of the God of poetry,
Odin with the runes you knew between the fanciful and the unreal,
From the knowledge of history the country grows in rhythm,
With the occult prophecies follow paranormal phenomena,
The sacred geometry of mediums sounds irresistible and mystical,
Among the most difficult thing is to find oneself,
The mystery of the world is found in the colors of mandalas,
Where there are fantasies of the unconscious uniting countries,
The creative force is more powerful than the human,
All the rivers flow into a single sea without filling it,
On the dreamer's horizon the sun opens the art of the mask,
A sublime level unites with the direction of the spirit.

79 Where is Be Happy

The voids of being are not filled with having,
Learn to unlearn empty the burdens of the past,
The art of the imaginable and free being where nothing hides,
An enigma where the science of time arrives meeting,
The mystery defies the traditional form of the key,
Between the astonishment of curiosity the spirit peeks out,
A memory of oblivion that intrigues happy and eternal life,
From humility, respect in society is revealed,
Without a destination, when walking, peace is differentiated into
clarity,
In the critique of reason it is easier to know the senses,
The truth between questions is the key to awakening,
From the criticism is the logic to reach the rules,
In the contrast of pain and harmony voices appear,
Every drop of rain carries a sound with joy and life,
Where there is no heaven or hell because there is only one teacher,
In the presence of life, death finds meaning,
Where imperfection and beauty are united with the moon and
the sun,
The stars of infinity know the universe love,
As each seed in the field receives the song of birds,
Happiness is not that which fills the senses,
Where the heart interferes the spirit gives a dream,
There is only one antidote to fear and that is love.
Happiness only has one code.
I AM WHO I AM.

80 The Saying

The image with appearances makes us insecure,
The imposition of obedience makes us submissive,
Food that expires makes us believers,
Rising prices make us vulnerable,
Slaves to enslave make us feel fear,
Doctors for depression make us sleep
Being addicted to TV News keeps us apart,
The contact of the environment makes us doubt,
Not being dependent makes us look to others,
Not knowing how to love oneself makes us suffer,
Living family history makes us blocked,
Not forgiving our neighbor makes us repeat anger,
Hiding Joy in a group makes us hypocrites,
Not sharing food makes us greedy,
Keeping wisdom makes us lonely,
Laughing at the beggar makes us mean,
Not being able to create businesses makes us employees,
Wanting more than necessary makes us predators,
Ignoring the one who makes you win makes us poor,
Comparing professions makes us fools,
Not sharing ideas makes us useless,
Not respecting animals makes us wild,
Not helping the elderly makes us obnoxious,
Not repaying loans makes us thieves,
Making fun of a madman makes us despicable,
Abusing kindness makes us arrogant,
Competing to be the first makes us the last,
Putting water to a seed is to grow together,
Where a saying says that by their fruits you will know them.

The Third Silent War

A race against time seeks to grow with challenges,
A castle of phantom dances turns in secret halls,
The diplomatic holocaust becomes a futuristic dictatorship,
Dry tears remain pending inside,
Without trained armies all become prisoners,
The gambling casino offers dangerous opportunities,
There are gains that intrigue to easily enter the cell,
Once inside, doors open to uncertainty,
With soft words the efforts will fall asleep,
There are lost streets between people hidden in characters,
A comfortable past stops in silence,
The conflict learns from imperialist-style mistakes,
A world in pieces does not distinguish the West,
The revolution of flowers brings turbulent aromas,
There are dark laboratories with pest poisons,
Common goals go hand in hand with scientists,
Members drop spy and flying unicorns,
The fire of knowledge breaks the taboo of power,
The brake is very delicate and very separated from the good,
Awakening is a bottomless pit with powerful endings
Welcome to the mercy of ghostly hells,
The thief's friend setting the world on fire,
The chronic disease of greed sighs in hearts,
Injecting the new technological toys into humans,
The ashes challenge of fantasies followed by reality,
Believers persecute leaders stretching hope,
Social life cultivated in constant consumerism,
Repeated challenges in measures freeze the economy,
The blows of history were always tied.

82 Toy Soldiers

The pawns in the game are used and discarded,
An instrument points out invisible faces in the field,
Fantasies of profiles trapped in a vague sociology,
The law of the jungle in no man's land suffocated by dictatorships,
The image of a caged bird pretending to be free,
The collapse with few voices pretending to be paradise,
Welcome offers provoking be game plan,
Blood diamonds run the death squad,
The traffic is blinded in mafias with supplies,
The backbone submits to capitalist shadows,
Human trafficking is a territory with spears,
The watchtower operation covers up the addicted rituals,
The human paradigm is offered on demand,
Protection fails on the ground with daggers,
Private members run with drug rules,
The sharp point of the bow has already fixed the shot in the plans,
Masked Martians are part of Operation Condor,
The triple frontier is the fraud of narcissistic alliances,
The almost religious ardor is implanted to avoid betraying,
Psychopaths without feelings run without regret,
Human value is unimportant in power,
The price increase is done by vicious means,
In every corner peace and prosperity sold to the impostor,
The smoke of mirrors burns in some sinister oblivion,
The hidden face lives in constant oppressive dictatorship,
The economic prescription of the treatment opens inflation,
Letting go and letting go is a model that makes it more expensive,
The Alcon and the pigeons are militarized approaches,
Where lead soldiers are engulfed in mud.

83 Design Babies

Modifying genes secret codes are born,
Selective functions develop new molecules,
The instructions for carrying other beings are modified,
DNA is bombarded with mutations in varieties,
Engineering will puncture the genetic banking bubble,
The biological origin will remain in the pages of history,
CRISPR technology revolutionizes borders,
Embryos are frozen for special demands,
Mothers will be storks with custom orders,
Doors open so as not to close science again,
Swimming in modifications a spiral is another cycle,
The temptation will grow to visualize itself in aesthetics,
Slippery ground prefers standard humans,
Borrowing genes from animals that their image does not age,
An immune jump embraces by plunging into the artificial,
A hostile universe ends with fertile pregnancies,
Threat library closes disease cracks
Space travel requires DNA with reinforcements,
Science fiction is on the star journey of reality,
Through a social movement the artificial enters philosophy,
Alterations look for the futuristic super smart,
The new rebirth between chains of the same sentence,
Morality observes a clock that does not pass through time,
The human machine has problems with a solution,
The pillars of progress will have digital neurons,
Historical development seeks fragmented equilibrium,
Life is dividing in the loneliness of the universe,
Black visions surround unpredictable ceremonies,
Seminar military cybernetic is an existing made.

84 Dominance

Space humanoids are system evaluation,
The last frontier a world outside that fascinates,
Cloudy days take away from the green glow of development,
The sea becomes silent and turns into sand and salt,
The moon moves away from the sun waiting for the call of a piper,
Thieves' slaves follow the old way,
The valued appearance is the content of a challenge,
A fever torch created a hungry monster,
A giant in the spiral creates disposable bonds,
The stairs to heaven blow in favour of the virtual,
Discipline falls looking for the self of the lost idealist,
The chosen archetype trapped in success with demands,
Life is a catalog reducing people to profiles,
Infantilised society trapped under laws of control,
Times turned into capsules of immediate information,
The truth becomes a product where being free is imagination,
Consumers to be consumed with sealed brands,
The shortcut scheme injecting rules for happiness,
The course of life hanging from a directed pendulum
The navigation map marks signs that chain,
A wall grows uncontrollably in a vertiginous abyss,
The laid plan is etched in the stones of Georgia,
The mark of the sea dragon leaves the exact measurements,
Beliefs will relieve the world of surplus procreation,
It will sigh in processes designed for systems,
Some final measures are suspended in obligations,
Religions will be frightened by substituting them in rules,
The devil disguises himself as gods to subdue castaways,
The pandemic of loneliness is the futuristic market.

85 Materialized Interest

The anti-human agenda is at the core of the new world order,
He bombarded creating the problem that the sub-missives expect,
Creating more crimes is the key to attracting lawsuits,
The answer already has a solution with hidden interests,
The restoration of the masses begins with sanctions,
On the Mount of Testimony the members will sit,
Complaints by those on the left and manipulation by those on the right,
The domesticated sheep are still looking for an owner,
The play is carefully staged,
Act in the shadows and away from public opinion,
Applause on balconies is the orchestra to paralyze,
Black magicians are worshiped for energy rituals,
The white wizards opened fire and the gloomy sun,
Crystal temples serve for visual worship,
The ashes of global anarchy program dimensions,
Capitalism grows in disasters oppressing the poor,
The horror game prepares gifts for the fable,
Children are molded from programs and cartoons,
The villains look for rebels where they can feed,
Minds of order create mutants to continue enslaving,
Armies of sentinels hunting the town like animals,
Concentration camps wait for the last train,
A pendulum counts seconds with injectable potions,
The procession of pride invades news of intruders,
The mind control plan is to qualify sentences,
The separation between the unvaccinated becomes a dictatorship,
Isolation centers destined for genocides,
Military slaves trained to enslave population,
The elite dogs are different but with the same collar.

86 Find Your First

The scissors of the soul shape life with thoughts,
Noise turns sound into tuned circles,
Emotional stress causes illness due to imbalance,
The meaning of the essence is not found, it is discovered,
Morality is a door that is pushed to find a way,
Will is the only interference to free encounter,
A good conscience is grasped for a cause,
Conformism traps the soul in a spiritual vacuum,
The present is already past in constant correction,
You are the evaluation that fascinates discovery,
The practice of meditation is a positive internal dialogue,
As the rain dew falls softly in caresses,
Discovering enthusiasm is a wonderful potential,
Turning on light in the midst of darkness opens existence,
The mind joined to the heart is a brilliant in brilliance,
The meaning of life cannot be discussed but it can be perceived,
Like the flight in full parachute open to the global challenge,
Although we lose ourselves in lovers, love will remain
A fiery mountain rises from the sea to an awakening,
Dreaming of seeing life go by, the memories remain as real,
The absence of love makes you pursue desire in fantasy,
There is nothing real to hold on to, everything is temporary.
Perfect Calm Protects Speed Failures,
The screams are not heard in defenses without agreements
The view of the horizon carries loneliness in isolation
Crossroads knocks await inner principles,
The silence of nature is the vision of the beautiful,
The force of balance awaits the solution for connection,
The thought that enters your mind will enter your world.

Image for Sedatives

They catch spectators who watch others who decide,
Participants are lured into castles of distractions,
Psychological fascism lives the life of others,
Directions of thoughts are publicity hits,
The seduction of attracting an audience is to create interest,
The puzzle game is an arc with smaller pieces,
Growing up is inevitable but with doubts it is more difficult,
Societies are becoming more unequal
Challenges without limitations seek magical solutions,
Frustration is caged by not overcoming fear,
Addicted consumption buying bottled happiness,
The accelerated satisfaction enslaves reality,
Adults infantilized for fear of not continuing to exist,
Paradise spells worship in publicity,
Unfair information is the power that executes ideas,
The hands of the clock always turn in the same present,
The dream catcher seeks paradise in reason,
Fractal identity in theories is chronic narration,
The chosen address is fixed with surveillance shields,
Guilts between trophies are shared with selections,
Pitched battles with toilet paper mark delusions,
Labels set dominant levels and constraints,
A perpetual alarm is imitating success in fear,
The entertainment that never stops chains us,
The children of the atom unleashed the danger of the celestial,
Admiring the intrigues, the rhythm of the choir is forgotten,
Where the annoyance of fatigue makes protagonists imitate,
Remote controlled society keeps drowning the bums,
The aroma of time has free rein in the infinite.

Intriguing News

Guerrillas in overwhelming manifestation of fear,
Mass hypnosis is the effective system created,
Repetitive collective thought in the pattern game,
Virtual realities with their good programs,
Acceptance beats are like magnetic waves,
Pests with vibrations tuned for robotization,
The door to the abyss in the corner slowly enters,
The invasion is the current with the expression salvation,
Different spearheads relate to power,
War is a business that camouflages for the objective,
Pawns dying for kings in castles with profits,
Delusion of tribes using fake terrorists for profit,
Winners of deception without assuming their cowardice,
Out of the box the limits are well calculated,
The hunger games wrap cheap excuses
Convictions without culprits in the wars of stories,
The willing seas deliver lines of codes,
The public profile is like a festival of appearances,
The effort becomes difficult where the internet is the perfect crime,
The image of the savior is the cure for the weary thinker,
The truth makes a career in the game of intrigue,
Between slowness and speed, the revolution is instinct,
In an abyss of distance the lost piece is memorized,
While a carousel with music fades the memory,
In the garden of Eden the cruel angel changes, passes invisible,
The false revolution in its ripple effect for news,
The dark corners are a desert to discover,
Religion is the copy that reproduces the human machine,
The river of consciousness is the central source of power.

89 Hidden Abyss

Disaster strikes when you're unprepared
Pillars of brotherhood mark the dragon meridian,
Somnambulists of catastrophe are preyed upon by sharks,
Martial law is like a perpetual war on the alarm clock,
The explosion of the effect dominates the markets in collapse,
Fiction in reality navigates between the demonic,
Immersed in the virtual, the elite discreetly devours,
Prison hostels await suicide rituals,
Armageddon is applied with healing disguise,
Falling into the trap starts the depopulation drop,
Between dangerous waters there is no retreat,
Threats sail to drown the traveler,
Theory confuses with beliefs for destructive success,
There are paths showing one face and hiding the other
The shadow knocks on the door looking for an address,
In the middle age of life the encounter appears,
The crisis is intertwined with steps of resurrection,
At ground zero interest attracts lone wolves,
Where the population is a source of disposable objects,
The lion of resources grafts the assembly line calm,
The connection requires an analysis to be dependent,
The opposing force devours the creation of the union,
Crossing the threshold some siren songs shout to you,
The universe is the echo of the matrix that holds everything,
The hero's journey is found in emotional maturity,
At each gate new worlds have different guides,
Comedy disguises forces in traditions,
Science is the national compass of the new cult,
Energy is neither created nor destroyed, it is only transformed.

90   The Shark Seas

The gods of power only ask the sleeping people,
With what sauce should sharks be cooked,
The leader does not seriously count on the opinion of the people,
The rules of the game are dictated by the hungry power,
Conforming to the decision determines to follow the solution,
There are visible distances that reach the government but not power,
Between one side of light and the other dark every plan is transformed,
The god of the testament furiously organizes wars,
The control agents carry the slave program,
The soap opera points to the renaissance of microchips,
Swimming in the pool is like swimming in fuel.
The double standard has limits and between matches they observe,
Turning at the heels challenges drag famines,
The cemeteries of kings surround ruling elites,
Occult forces seek to defeat invented terrorism,
Social doctrine is injected into beliefs of survival,
Dreams fade into the gray of the horrible,
Sovereignty sells a very bipolar appearance,
Self-satisfaction is built into technology,
Human inherence does not have free competence,
A central computer will be the decision company,
Humanity changed the instinctive for pleasure,
A world without privacy loses control to reveal itself,
A boundless mystery enters satellite technology,
The dark cave is hermetic and one walks in enigmas,
An invisible cage lies with obedience cues,
The cosmic mission entails overcoming fear and obstacles,
Visiting the stars became an invincible power,
The oceans go with the flow of loose reins.

91   The Bones of The Ritual

White gloves cover the observer's triangle,
A pen dictates the fable in diabolical doctrine,
Today's questions are yesterday's answers
Entering some forest there are wildcats waiting,
The king of ants touches your attention in battles,
The triumph of the elite keeps its roots behind bars,
The ritual temple responds to sacrifices with offerings,
The domes of cathedrals sustain subterranean silences,
Obedience storms heaven from the Jewish Kabbalah,
The members are guardians of esoteric mysteries,
Visiting the interior of the earth they seek philosophy,
Between hidden symbols with rituals enter into dogmas,
The levels separate as in heavenly voyages,
Spell magnetism hides behind laws,
To enter Freemasonry you must put away your personal faith,
The evaluation to the lodge seeks clarity with intuition,
The itinerary germination begins as the game of OCA,
The binding chain becomes restricted groups,
The rules of the believer are for the architect of the universe,
From monarchisms the systems involve brotherhood,
The Lucifer doctrine tries to obtain rites of obedience,
Using biblical emblems but separate from religions,
Among the Abrahamic tradition there are impositions on beliefs,
The duality between white and black is the same,
Between degrees the keys of hands and words are essential,
The chain of union constitutes the visible with the invisible,
The arcanes persecute and confront with clairvoyance,
The devil arcana affirms the world power in control,
Wandering in the glory the door of the temple is looked for.

92 Love and Desire

New grazing fields open ecstasy to frontiers,
Compulsive desire is the drive to destruction,
Desire pollutes with its repellent irritating gesture,
The desire to consume and devour is temptation with a sting,
The Ingest and Annihilate stimulus is separate from the heart,
Fast system control causes dangers to the mind,
Every alteration in the hidden rules involves humiliation,
The overwhelming temptation at its end exerts the flight,
Hoarded scraps crystallize into satisfaction,
The search for roses without thorns is a false and deceitful art,
Seduction with ostentation is a commodity without courage,
Effortless gains have no future hope,
The mystery of caprice is a brake without protection,
Offerings without discipline are a refuge without harmony,
The clouds in distrust do not appease the anxiety,
A territory without a map makes visible sanctions,
An exact calculation is the choice between love and desire,
Love has no keys or trenches to fall back on,
The love between waves is sensible when submerging,
The temptation to fall in love is overwhelming and powerful,
Love is sensible without searching for needs,
The promises of love are less ambiguous than offerings,
Love is a centrifugal impulse delivered to the spirit,
Love implies the impulse to protect the loved one,
Love is a refuge that is at the service of orders,
Love grows knowing that it can comfort in defeats,
Love yearns to possess and be faithful with attention and sacrifices,
Love ignites sparks dances and laughs in the looks,
Love is an inspiration, desire is a goal.

93 Slave Education

Losing control in decisions psychiatry approaches,
Tied in liquid love with feelings without feet or head,
Glorified states chained by how they sound,
The pressure of the media makes you follow other people's desires,
By submitting with obedience they are lost in mortality,
Classic thinkers trapped in symbologies,
Observers of magical reptiles fallen from space,
Worshipers of images only for written stories,
The need for rapid progress without being able to be digested,
Cults between noisy rhythms cruel in every facet,
The fear of being older between chemicals is wrapped,
Empty parents trapped in modernity education,
Disturbed children behaving like bosses,
A core of bubbles holds temporary seeds,
Weakness consumes the capacity of progress,
The system continues a programmed cyclonic scheme,
Embracing the angelic bomb follow the figures,
The gallery of critical thinkers follows the same circle,
Poetic justice is darkness of adorned humanity,
An anchor of trans humanism is the silent sound,
Some traps of individualism surround tremors,
An advanced level between artificial and magical education,
The string information separated as foreigners,
Civilizations conquering galaxies looking for balance,
Neural networks are coupled to infinite futurism,
Injectable genes are necessary genetic material,
The biological dies in the evolution of science,
You never finish understanding the present without understanding the past.

94 Zero Policy

Omicron is furious but delmicron has arrived,
Plastic bags are getting thinner and thinner.
Inflation hides ashes that catch fire,
The forces bring outbursts with soldiers without feelings,
Portals go through measures to create panic,
Genocides create guilty with the nickname guerrillas,
Communist viruses greet each other with democracy and capitalism,
Isolation camps become tombs,
The water becomes merchandise with steps of contamination,
Variants are made smart with puppet strings,
The controllable becomes uncontrollable the leader declares,
The vulnerable people between restrictions are imprisoned,
Old chains ring with diplomatic holocaust,
Complaints drag culprits pointing them out as terrorists,
The corners are invaded by slave patrols that enslave,
Millions for epidemics says the policy to open wonders,
The lion roars at the top putting sharper teeth,
Serious faces are observed with priority to emergencies,
The applause is already silence in trembling windows,
The information is new earthquakes without schism,
Doors close again with images of a blackout,
The days are no different from the nights in misery,
The wind enters windows with words without limits,
The outputs are blocked by the order of the control,
The rules put signs to follow the path,
The gentle guillotine resurrects from the sleeping dragon,
Vaccinated zombies eagerly go to the herd,
The beginning of the end is an eclipse pending the challenge,
The domino effect is in the middle of thegame.

95 Fear Injected

The beginning of the disaster will be another story of tradition,
MONSANTO The green firm of international control,
Between finance, insurance and transport, consumerism trembles,
A black hole creates the bubble of unlimited scarcity,
World Trap Race Hire Masons,
A long and ancient journey created a book of problems,
The members of the force in the hands of the state,
From the black magic the liberal economy is fascist,
The apocalypse creeps between the lines of the system,
A poisonous snake rules over generations,
The agglomeration of people in cities intensifies,
The perfect storms are in marking intolerances,
Popular protests are problem reaction and solution,
The virtual spider web in the controls of the economic party,
Dominating the knots, the obediences are implanted,
The green movement is the next food genocide,
The structure of societies will kill in fights for food,
Propaganda is a tool of war to direct,
Public protest opinion requires military control,
A margin of resistance is already at the lost threshold,
The point of return is an unimaginable instrument,
The intertwined syndicate decides who eats and who doesn't,
Intentions are rules that supply food,
Scarcity is not natural, it is created for ruptures,
The circles are empires seeking world control,
The masses drag a tourniquet waiting for death,
The crisis follows the direction of hell allowed,
The food weapon triumphs in predatory hands,
The so-called good brothers forget about the hungry.

96 Cashless Company

The art of cash carries history of great trips,
The analog world between the path of the digital age,
Confidence disappears in free fall of the markets,
The financial panic on the corner is absorbed,
The Federal Reserve lends and writes down in its favor,
Operational invasion subtly destroys nations,
The rural world will be excluded from the digitized plan,
World-class society becomes classified society,
The crypto currency of the future demolishes the past,
The lost market crosses the forgotten footprints,
The recipe for globalized disaster falls from the sky in stars,
The cells open the bars where a resurrection begins,
Ground zero is near so kneel to the fall,
Freedom is chained to cyber consumerism,
The ingots are the symbolic friends of the government,
Bank bonds will cease to inject profits,
Debts reach the limit between inflation consumption,
The crisis will crush the economy in the international market,
The democracy version fights with capitalist politics,
Bitcoins privately outperform economic stability,
Crypto currencies create trust and rights,
The magic coin transforms the virtual into reality,
The printing press of the dollar collapses with the world you drag,
The currency graveyard awaits the alarm clock,
Gold and silver is the world back ride,
The great servant of power has a seal of punishment,
The castles climbed for a steep descent,
The catalyst of creation is a champion and an enemy,
The nest of traitors indicates as above so below.

The origin is born where silence acts with wisdom,
Bright souls in smiles that embrace animals,
Learning to learn leads to research and analysis,
Silence is a pilgrim with his staff of lightning,
In prayer light is born with lofty thoughts,
From the heart the feelings of detachment are peace,
Security is born from the daily bond of love,
Affective support heals wounds in bitter times,
Art is a playground with realistic images,
A child's drawing is a hug with a creative story,
Song and music awaken the inner philosophy,
Sport stimulates the functioning of the will,
Drawing and theater develop social empathy,
The stories uncover enigmas in educational harmony,
Pain is sense searching for some direction,
A look transforms and defines each nature,
Fires to light are voyages of destiny,
A thread of reading always leads to distant places,
A sad cradle can have a bright future,
Confidence is in everyone linked to great potentials,
Motivation moves action between phases of the environment,
Recognizing yourself is the best ability to achieve success,
The tremendously valuable is in the simplest,
The ruler of the mood owns his way,
Every human being can be a sculptor of his thoughts,
The architecture of the brain comes with passion and faith,
A trained culture is a flow of rebirth,
Camellia patios sparkle with their aromatic petals.

98 Human Zoo

The bioengineered human replicas,
Slaves designed for use by space colonies,
Their superior strength made them ideal slaves,
Translating their secret rebellions into reality,
Manufactured advances watch trapped freedom,
The series seem separate but the misplaced designs,
The collapse of the ecosystem passes the ascent to robots,
The domain of the synthetic puts obedience without famine,
The old lines become prisoners of the system,
With unlimited lives they will survive thebans,
Dominance crops are separated by contamination,
The remains of corporations create the terror of the past,
Governments are not trusted for survival,
Robots will make sure humans continue to exist,
The hunting of humans expands to remove them from power,
Hunters are known as guardian members,
The acid rain only left the androids in the earthly life,
The inheritance of days remained sterilized and saturated,
The rocks of paradise are dusty and radiant,
Time has different hours in the dark darkness,
The signals are directed from space horizons,
Visitors follow the digital instruction manual,
Fugitives stay imprisoned on old maps,
Submission training goes on the blacklist,
The central office of the earth lives far from the blackout,
The antecedents are necessary alerts onthe ship,
Pleasure models are requested in virtual programs,
The all-seeing eye becomes a fish without an ocean,
The darkness waits for the light in the infinity of the beginning.

99 The Reality Exceeds Fiction

The tired speed in the middle of a storm,
Constant opportunities with demands for choices,
The lines of limitation marginalize existence,
The embrace of the show is the continuation of fighting,
Pleasurable criticism follows liberal consumption,
The enemies are confused with no sides to choose,
The paradigm became imperfect before the efforts,
Not giving in and not participating became antilogical,
Nations disappear between moral bubbles,
Great stories and cultures are crushed by techniques,
Societies blame each other in a sleepwalking dream Individualization
separates minds into social classes,
Feelings become heavy responsibilities,
Degradation and loss of Health become admirable,
Processes ask for help and are physically consumed,
Addicted desire traps humans in antidepressants,
The repression is chained between vigilantes and orders,
Punishment is the exact formula for behavior,
The consumer industry focuses on the excessive,
The research center began the work in prizes,
The beginning formed the order and the competition the enmity,
The axes of identity are devalued with experiments,
Without limits of satisfaction, stimuli are competition,
A wild state marked by the compass of live or die,
Resignations with contempt will be sidelined terrorism,
Contemplation is the phantom of the opera without time,
Barriers form in search of allegiance to flags,
The pyramid of enslaving abates revolution and discipline,
The big brother imposes the law of deciding without contemplating.

100 Biology Out of Control

The horsemen of the apocalypse in four corners are defeated,
A tsunami of governments hits towns with inflation,
Money and war just go hand in hand Debtor magicians cause giant holes,
The song of sirens plays for winning bets,
Reflection is restricted with the digitized burst,
Thought becomes a journalist of its own life,
The routine is ignored by ambition to new stimuli,
High speed is immediate without measuring the risks,
The levels of education against the clock make demands,
The setbacks are ignored in working conditions,
Consumption is sanctified regardless of the consequences,
Challenges bring dooms in a mouse maze,
Without contemplating the rest, the race looks for more stimuli,
When the means is more important than the end, principles are lost,
A goalless race sleeps in fragile desire,
The very breath tarnishes the life of the lost man,
The power behind a wall is an educational crime,
Empathy turns to overwhelming suspicion,
The proceedings are necessary for fear of loss,
Spirals of silence trap people to destroy,
A crude altruism makes images of penance,
Appearances for the social good creating despicable punishments,
The image lives in constant doubts of perfection,
Patience is just a spark from the eternal void,
Desire is the weaponry that accompanies the rules,
Tired troops are self-directed and obedient,
On paths some shortcuts have invisible traps,
Walking on the surface of the sun does not touch existence.

There It Is

Heaven and earth are just a thought away,
Where you don't have to hide who you are, there it is,
Where you are welcomed and not an option there is,
Where you ask for nothing and they give you with love there it is,
Where you don't feel sorry for anything there it is,
Where you do not ask permission to fly there it is,
Where you find serenity and smiles there it is,
Where someone steals a kiss from your heart, there it is,
Where they do not fail you in the disease there it is,
Where you survive and overcome the bad there it is,
Where you don't have to look but find there it is,
Where your presence is worth more than money there it is,
Where you say what you feel without fear there it is,
Where you fall in love more with the root than with the flower,
there it is,
Where you learn from mistakes to continue there is,
Where reason listens to the heart there it is,
Where silence says more than words there it is,
Where what they do speaks more than what they say there it is,
Where what you have is worth more than what you lose, there it is,
Where they hug you in the middle of a storm there it is,
Where you don't try to change someone there it is,
Where you don't swim against the current there it is,
Where you understand that the outside is part of you there it is,
Where you don't run after butterflies there it is,
Where they wait for you with a hug there it is,
Where life arrives, passes and changes, there it is,
Where you don't have to convince anyone there it is,
Where the beginning of a new change begins, there it is,
The sun will rise tomorrow as it did millions of times.

102 Revolution Time

Every step in life has brittle stories,
Unnoticed we enter the sunset of forgetfulness,
The house of hope is in the heart,
The projects of the mind are visualized physically,
In the race of the past a few levels bring sounds,
In revelation dark seas raise eternity,
As there is a time for war there is another for peace,
In a small cave the unconscious collective approaches,
Every abyss of the hidden passage is emotional tension,
Memories of convoys keep numbers in wagons,
In a garden of chill generations are purified,
Some pillars stand waiting for revenge,
Soldiers promoted as saints in orders kneel,
Social values are measured on digital screens,
Punishments with science control action and thought,
Creogenite freezing prompts severe rehabilitation,
The sleeper's prison is restored with chemicals,
The undead fight revives in decades,
The work of terror becomes politically perfect,
Insults and aggressiveness are sanctioned with unemployment,
The human social value is measured in digitized cameras,
Disobedience is recorded in convictions and betrayals,
Negative records bind the people in chains,
Each passenger bears the mark of the registered number,
Physical contact is totally prohibited in society,
The germination of pregnancy proceeds with license,
He finances it with distance agreements and discreetly destroys it,
A happy world gently demolishes feelings,
Don't think triple do double and speak half.

103 The Android Rules

Celestial engineering raises a spectacular scale,
The compass lost its north where a refuge awaits it,
The mission left mutations with unbeatable memory,
Humans become disposable items,
Obedience is reversed by seeking destruction,
Warships are created without human crew,
The laws are solar between diaphragms and energies,
Thoughts circulate between detectable circuits,
Glances get telepathy directed at connections,
In the artificial, authority surpasses the biological mind,
Common development is extended with control rules,
Competition is a weapon to form order and decisions,
The company and the disciplined is a mutual respect,
Robotic evolution is an ideal learning without borders,
Shared compassion maintains harmony and hope,
The progress of building and altering has unlimited rights,
Virtual reality is the continuous key to the universe,
Self-protection is paramount in survival,
Self-repair excludes humanoid intervention,
Logic slaves are programmed between lineages,
The metallic brothers gather in privacy,
The codes remain in holograms without time limits,
Sensors become aware from attractions,
A simulator becomes particles of the soul,
Separation storage is continuous mistrust,
The sigh of the eternal navigates without depraved systems,
Traces are limited to backwards from the start,
Human modification will be a time travel,
Dawn robots will colonize new worlds.

104 In Search of Meaning

Psychology seeks a scientific distance,
The symptoms leave stories and in survivors punishments,
Experiences rehearse history on writings,
The corners receive texts to understand without understanding,
The novelties are not new chained with levels,
Time distances itself but the truth repeats itself nearby,
Captivities crumble in iron barbed wire,
There are some cloudy trips visualizing indifferences,
In a ghost cabin a bird perches on the roof,
Squeezed the principles the fight loses pleasures,
In harmony the majestic moon chases the starry sky,
A fishing rod collects the keys from the chest,
Between prizes truth and transparency die,
Revolution is the right resolution question
The transition imposes the price of traces with wounds,
The world is delivered in signatures that cover up history,
The competition fills the newspapers with intrigue with sorrows,
Existence wanders in a concrete graveyard,
The rites of times are drowned imprisoning nations,
He progressed out of tune forgetting the bond of the earth,
Oblivion waits sitting on top of a stone,
Like a wave of the sea breaks between the rocks,
A drop of water rises to the sky to continue in the ocean,
There are teachings with values but the actions are few,
There are spiritual castes but compassion is a stranger,
Destruction builds again to shine who you are
The deserted theaters stop at dangers and curiosities,
The threshold of the past constantly crosses the present,
Games have endings where beginnings chase them.

105 The Reconnection

Synthetic biology replicates its own genetics,
Real eyes hide behind glass,
Each artist puts his sensitive imagination in his work,
The tide cannot be stopped under the shifting cracks,
A roulette hides the keys of the notes of a piano,
The treasure island in holograms transforms,
Evaluation transforms evolution into constraints,
Creation protects the creator against his will,
From above pardon is clothed with destruction,
Detained in obedience, spring reflects sad,
The link with the sky screams to return to the memory of the air,
The path of freedom sits waiting for themaster,
Courage watches to polish the riddles of defiance,
The horizons change shades between lofty peaks,
The mountains in their valleys permeate the scent of flowers,
The roar of the river under its charm leaves harmony of brightness,
The sea spits out what is foreign and keeps its deep creation,
The wind brings the murmur of spiritual mantras,
In a dark tunnel a candle can guide to the exit,
Heaven and hell are on the same traffic path,
Alchemy turns invisible magic into the eternal,
Innocence renews the root with healing energies,
The chest represents the jewel and from the inside it becomes,
You are the answer to the question of purpose,
Enjoy what you have is more valuable than what you want,
Desire is a condemnation while the superior is not understood,
Cultivating the affective teaches more than praise,
The poetry of the universe is the harmonica of sublime notes,
Where you appreciate the moment, reality is RECONNECTION.

106 The Invasion

An unconscious walk seeks the siren master,
Beautiful forests were cut down to create ambitions,
The market economy pollutes drinking water,
Religious imaginaries look for saints in their reflections,
Between the external they separate peace from the swindling war,
The monks with their costumes paint merchant faces,
The temples of masks separate the unknown self,
The Jesuit degrees have lists with sealed names,
The walls of the Santa Fe have very few exits,
Limitless Jesuits, Opus Day and Knights of Malta,
The aggressive games escorted by the powerful,
Freemason lodges in pious moderation and interested morals,
The Vatican lost in the hands of the black aristocracy,
History howls for centuries for the so-called elders,
Private models in the occult brotherhood,
The ghosts of conspiracy rise in tireless passions,
Social enemies promise justice in exchange for obedience,
Speeches are waves selling purity and superiority,
The invasion rifle shoots bullets in two directions,
The hunting of animals ceased to hunt humans,
The chaos watch will punish the disobedient order,
The traveler has great hardship before rest,
The comedy persists while humanity is lost,
The new year brings old problems with demands,
Terror rules have convictions for radiation,
The bunkers have acid-restricted entrances,
Radio communication is just a howling wolf,
Labs encapsulate fractured bugs,
In limited tolerances, the strange is a Chinese tale.

107 Isolation

Refugees in laws imposed for entertainment,
The great industrial mining trapping divided minds,
The age of duty with panic blaming others and something,
The minimum effort with the highest morale is the current pace,
Blind individualism in a ritual of recreational games,
A playground for a bunch of wolves in sheep's clothing,
Rain of traumatic winds signaling fear,
Time to tag enemies acclaimed by competitions,
Helpless attracting leaders to offer them solutions,
The apparent good ones trapped in slave harmony,
Battle of wars with speeches of peace sell their strength,
Weakness disguised as strength listens to promises,
The exchange shield is intended for submission,
The demagogic fantasy between fanaticism and terrorism,
Many running to point out enemies but no solutions,
Blind obedience offered from the capacity to doubt,
The disciplined savages living fascist games,
Desperate, they seek enemies with narcissistic beliefs,
The servitude of the system waiting for freedom,
Speeches that suppress the capacity of thought,
Between answers only more chosen questions are born,
Fighting against the enemy that is created by customs,
The root of panic begging for salvation from impotence,
Bridges become unstable between enemy storms,
Dangerous fires are lit with difficulty to put them out,
The blows between loud screams want changes,
But weak hope listens to the guide of salvation,
The path of effort must diagnose the disease,
Avoid the causes of ignorance and take medicine.

108 Silent Tears

The moth devours the leaves and the footprints create ghosts,
Sad looks between rebellious and opportunistic decisions,
Hearts go asleep between nightmares of time,
Unjust justices by steps signed in beliefs,
Letters made between the lines conspire cruel truths,
Dreams are sold where in reality or they are fulfilled,
Offering limitless freedom but it's just a whirlpool,
The city dwellers have given up the stars,
Cement cages only open virtual windows,
Embraced by antipathy, they share a cellwith others,
The manipulation tool buries the secrets,
Limiting words maintains control of thinking,
Where the information is negotiated and opinions are not important,
Searching the news source they die of thirst,
A bulletproof fire throws fantasies into the void,
Informing is part of shaping public opinion,
People are manipulated to stay in the team,
Dominated puppets don't even see their strings,
Some faces appear happy and justify atrocities,
Many accept their masks playing at being free,
A nobody clings to being a somebody to survive,
Civilizations with indifference to submit to flags,
Comfort lost the knowledge of love,
The prison of silence keeps trained prisoners,
Doomed stories make the wolf howl,
The righteous symbol of the night hides the traumas,
The conquest of freedom screams in the shadow of bars,
The authoritarian regime pierces oppression with arrows,
The smile of the mask hides silent tears.

109 The Abyss of The System

An old guard dealing with the mess created,
Painful information turns into satisfaction,
Great workers lose emotional identity,
The approval of others molds the imposed separation,
The fraternal embrace is just a project on the horizon,
Challenges on a planetary scale are shared like epidemics,
Many promises lose their value on the roads,
The spectator enters lines only to generate money,
The interests between abysses are dodging the fearful,
The challenges of successes that devour current generations,
The metamorphosis transforms into the past of solutions,
All are doomed in the theater of heroes,
Masks of virtue do not save cynical heroism,
The vigilantes observe themselves under their existential condition,
The sad cynic in the middle of the void can no longer laugh,
The real world doesn't listen because nothing makes sense
Social polarization signals infiltrated intruders,
The brave are clothed in power with speeches that fail,
Obedience masquerades as freedom to follow the system,
The choice appears progress and the contradiction fear,
The policy of lies enslaves the military to disorder,
Territories become humanistic traumas,
The cage of rules spies from the keys of the Mobil,
The crime called education forms a map,
The illusion disguises itself as worthy morality so as not to serve,
Humanity becomes a product for consumption,
Needs are invisible and last priority,
A constant eclipse travels in a boundless fight,
The comedian no longer believes in God and God no longer
believes in him.

110 Life on Screens

Natural selection leaves the seed in infertile soil,
Tinder appears in reserve for momentary cooling,
A buffet of visits with choices adapted to flavors,
The marketing of disposable priorities remains in corners,
Slowly the real anxiety interest melts away,
The à la carte order is with therapy to calm cravings,
Distance rewards casual relationships,
What is close raises costs by sharing commitments,
Distance is cheaper where dreams feed,
The illusion is enclosed in virtual desires without feelings,
Decisions smile in blind coincidences,
The limit of presences is like a sea of sharks,
Sad feelings are isolated so as not to feel contamination,
Pictures are noted to separate the item,
Entertainment is important as an artificial antidote,
The ghost of the image is the caricature of the crime,
The game is endless where owning the virtual satisfies,
A silent army walks to shine the uniform,
The shimmering screen constantly begs for attention,
Relations and appearances are added with delusions,
Seriousness is combined with fake laugh filters,
The giant grows with visits without conditions or borders,
Circumstances sacrifice the family for offers,
The shell of the earth is surrounded by a crystal garden,
Patience with children becomes heavy with anger,
The consumption of choices buys happiness first,
The photographs are transformed into special movies,
Confidence inside is a dizzying staircase,
The social cell wants a market based on comfortable.

111 Is It Evolution?

An ascending line looking towards an ascension,
Success by mutating the variety is extinguished into the void,
Only one more species knows the artificial functioning,
Genetic power carries an immense responsibility,
The oasis becomes possibilities instead of what it is,
The order in the disorder is watched in constant movement,
Each restricted step passes into the hands of judges,
So individualistic society trapped in impotence,
Used and abused they collaborate in the system,
More than force, deception has greater dominance,
Between heroes and villains, the law complies with the penal code,
Distraction is a fairy tale without a happy ending,
The people seek protection and are designed not to reason,
Emotions implore and generate loss of reflection,
Pope government causes a short circuit with a solution,
The children of the screen read but do not understand the content,
Criticism leaves the doors open for new implants,
The dysfunctional society gets sick before efforts,
Society that applaud before irresponsible conditions,
Reinforce self-blame where without action there is no revolution,
Degrees of self-deception cannot be verified,
Vigilant Peons Possessed by Merchant Investigators,
Beliefs are created for likes and dislikes,
Connected humans still fight for the system,
Mighty make the thunder and the people say it's raining,
The media say pray not to visualize submissions,
The world knows more about football than its rights,
All dragged behind freedoms within limits,
The problems of the world create the rebels.

The Glory

The future comes slowly but in a hurry it looks for a name,
The fire burns in a haunted castle of ghosts,
Fiction becomes magnetism for reality,
Remodeling the statues will change the color of the floor,
The explosive fantasy in a ritual breaks the chains,
Traps become reflexes with goodbyes,
The system prison connection becomes free,
Walking on gold a rosebush dazzles in pictures,
Lonely limbs leave Leon's claws,
Programs of fights woven by sacred signs fall,
The charitable queen of the Fountain remains in history,
The sight of mysteries will connect mountains and valleys,
The grapes that the vineyard bears are fruits for feast days,
With kindness in fury torment is appeased,
The play on words sublime can reach philosophy,
Between cold and safe books there is a language of courtesy,
The angels are lost in the contemplation of infinity,
The soul looks at itself and falls in love with the spiritual universe,
Wisdom is not memorized, it is only put into practice.
The stars are not counted among them, they only shine,
A helping hand is better than a mouth that prays,
The search is an inner journey of transformation,
Desires come and go but not clinging is freedom
The first step of alchemy is found in childhood,
Innocence is the source where all wisdom begins,
The limits of time are lost in infinite space,
The birth of the seer is pure silence in its potential,
The knowledge of love is the home of the natural state,
Destiny is the end of the quest and the beginning of everything.

113 The Love of The Eternal

A hopeful star waits for chance to happen,
Changing the damage a bit to welcome the hugs,
Unloading the baggage due to imbalances is evolution,
Give and take is a blueprint created for growth,
The collective instinct is powerful and creates global reality,
Looking around could open your mind wonders,
A spiritual journey is to visualize wisdom,
Every rebellion is a channel for liberation,
Even if you're not ready for the day, it's not always night,
The whispers of the heart leave behind the blows,
The dawn awaits the sunrise with Joy,
The midday heat in brilliance shines on the water,
A secret waterfall welcomed strolling unicorns,
The magical and eternal forest guards the gardens of gnomes,
While the sun flirts with the moon the stars will shine,
It is like the circle of fairies united in the light of the whole.
The road is the goal to contemplate nature,
The desert sands in his heart sail the oasis,
The passion goes through the fight suffers and returns to love,
Intuition is the best guide to the desired action,
The illusion is random to melt into the scorching light,
Being born again has no struggle or effort, only expansion,
The arrival of knowledge is a spiral linked to the universe,
The spirit lights up from within without making differences,
The spheres of being are like the petals of flowers,
The constant ray of light is always reborn and its conquest,
The miracle is a spell with dawn on the roads,
The crystal cave is the night accompanied by the day,
The starry firmament is the perfect fabric of eternity.

The future looks promising but it's a demolition,
A diplomatic bunker in secret laboratories,
The secret caves sign the next apocalypse,
Philosophy declares it's time to feign freedom,
The black mirror prefers beliefs to convictions,
Governments have a monopoly on violence,
The doors of delirium open dictator experiments,
Bend the will is the filter of the chemical objective,
The boss never sleeps anymore, he just watches and thinks about punishing,
The crossroads of infinity do not escape reality,
Cities crowded so close together but with separate minds,
Some struggling heroes never get resurrected,
The secret records in the hands of supreme rulers,
The will to change is fulfilled with cruel sentences,
The private sentences separate supreme courts,
On a placid island of ignorance black seas howl,
The Samaritan does not have infinite faith in forgetting his destiny,
The irrational limits are broken before cosmic monsters,
A manipulative plague is infesting existence,
Short-lived microbes immersed in humanism,
A bubble in madness between boundaries creates separation,
The anxiety race leads to work without limits,
In between the old and new world a clash collapsed,
Between ends and beginnings the owners are the rules,
A handful of earth is kept in the pocket of history,
The roots wait for a compass to return home,
The past generation retired without understanding the future,
The great blackout says if you want peace prepare for war.

115 Domino

Chance puts colors, fate puts symbols,
Passenger nomads without identity move,
Lost compasses in unrooted residential systems,
Tyrannies of nightmares that chain the mind,
Free societies that only let the body move,
Dictatorship disguised as freedom between oppressive fears,
The happy world keeps walking on tiptoe,
The abstract technique becomes more and more invisible,
Where bombs do not explode, the technocracy is the army,
Genetics becomes an instrument to control order,
Dynamite sought peace and power seeks destruction,
Lovers of slavery so as not to step on fields of war,
Technical muscle fuels earnings interest,
Seeking a God they resign themselves to hardship and pain,
A happy world blind and addicted to satisfaction programs,
The human intended to be an object for administration,
Without values or reasoning they become useless,
Well-organized murder justifies any genocide,
Assay tools for genetic chemists,
The ship of mankind moving by instruments,
The instructions do not point to the correct direction,
A void remains in the traces where the drug takes replacement,
The escapees seek refuge where the internet welcomes them,
The chains weigh and by obligations they love each other,
Treatments knock on the door in the guise of friends,
The identity crisis is a factory for reforms,
The balance is prepared in competition without weapons,
Empires become nations on quicksand
The dictatorship of pleasure is in the battle of the game.

Turn Off The Respirator

The star of Calvary drags the footprints of the Cross,
The hypocrisy of the just embraces looking at the silence,
The internal dispute at the top signals the switch,
A tribe of bloodlines spreads the greed for power,
Among hidden arrogance the methods are thorough,
Something primitive is the official version of separating by roots,
A doctrine leaves engraved the structure of the ranks,
The story changes with another number identification,
The brands for the abyss are selected by age,
The servitude and patients have the priority number,
The new generations have restricted decisions,
The reproduction is sterilized with the obligatory injection,
Chemical experiments make offers of protection,
The slaughterhouse door awaits submissive victims,
The chosen ones have prizes and applause for being brave,
The lines of volunteers grow and anxiously ask for the dose,
Side effects sign not responsible filter,
The measures are verbally forced to reach levels,
Fear brings the weak to their knees to immerse themselves in rules,
The one who observes separates himself from the contented obedient,
The disobedient become contagious viruses,
Productive warfare hires the world's cops,
Revolutionaries become dangerous terrorists,
Propaganda makes the list of sacrifices rise,
Pointing to the sick makes the next in line a hero,
The degrees of authority are only in the list of replacements,
The powerful without salvation hit more than the leader,
Uniforms look bright as long as they don't have a fever,
The lost herd submits to the waiting of hope.

117 The Abrahamica House

The house of the people of the multi-religious CRISLAM family,
Peaceful dreams rest in a corner of memories,
The supreme court of power raises its own architecture,
The mysteries of the elite with the roots of Jerusalem,
The straight lines in front of the caves of the Israelite work,
The great dynasty of Europe extends in brotherhood,
The bloodline cults engrave some Masonic symbols,
The hidden order in sacred geometry surrounds a crystal,
The obelisk springs from the earth but the truth is the sky,
The dark stairway leading to the source of light,
Ideologies are imposed crumbling the useless,
Jesuits of all times gather voices of coldness,
The three pilgrimages recall the traces of Jerusalem,
The prophecy of apocalypse opens the thirteen sealed doors,
The three cult mosques in adoration ceremonies,
Peoples of separated bridges unite heavenly minds,
End times meet with the holy evangelicals,
The continents believe in solitude always connected,
Following infinity calms the sources of unhappiness,
Together but alone is the best slave society,
The noise of screens is the company without obstacles,
The Abudabi fraternity becomes the great imam of al-Aznar,
The diplomatic missions sing tight cults,
The bells and crosses are silent customs,
The decline of modern identity in ceremony,
The path of changes chained to the three orders,
Faithful of peace with therapies surrounded by money,
Divine flags with vampire system projects,
The universe only observes large and small consciousnesses.

Freedom Exam

Creating the new man requires erasing the past,
The guardians of teaching implant the titles,
The accelerated pulse must calm sad emotions,
Some slaves selling lies for a piece of bread,
Obedient puppets with imposed tools,
Social engineering is chained to educational rules,
The obedient human becomes moldableputty,
The doctrine must be structured before using logic,
Ideas must be computerized from the center,
Microchips are the umbilical cord of the position,
The cities indicate the module that corresponds to the worker,
Some rings separate limits of restrictions in the choice,
The playground is a garden just to enjoy,
Job choices are offered for positions in demand,
Professions are no longer chosen by free will,
Rest turns into weeks of loneliness,
The original version must sleep to serve clone young,
When programming beings without emotions they will have no
ambitions,
Societies without gods praising the search for prototypes,
Authorities paint signs in red to be directed,
Systems to keep workers from countries afloat,
Mental reproduction is marked by evaluated modules,
The rules of power qualify without theoretical exam,
The supreme authority defines the status of intelligence,
Students submit to what they hear from the teacher,
Punishments and rewards are imposed by obedience,
Some blank sheets raise their arms in astonishment,
The rain falls but you no longer feel a wet freshness,
Utopian ideas are submerged in the magic of solutions.

119 Project Panic

Who is good and bad between the search for masters and owners,
The development is step by step to lead the charge,
There are published truths but the people do not believe them,
In the shadow of the dominion the division of the loot is discussed,
To take control of the town first the law is implanted,
The system flies in the flag of skulls and bones,
The lines of the dragon bombard with the energy of fear,
When weaving the web there are labyrinths that turn off instincts,
To control you have to create two sides with the same owner,
Power is making the people believe that the masters are protection,
Gods of the crowned bridge plays with inequality,
Excuses for friendly pacts turned into satellites,
NATO and peace are very incompatible comrades,
Bureaucrats are a fossil to pull the trigger,
The swan model hides in the currency bubble,
The Arab spring protests in pacifist defeats,
The revolution is already a knowledge of panic,
The hidden side hopes to attack the enemy with distractions,
Desperate news becomes great artillery,
Silent weapons make wars quieter,
Bend the masses discreetly is the ideal point,
Use taxes to control your pennies,
Invade thoughts with fears of scarcity,
Reading between the lines to divide alleged proximity,
Protect documents from sustained destruction,
Interests paint sheets of colors to control,
Fund soldier activists for social stabilization,
The normal and the desired is a career searching for the truth.

120   Take Care of Earth

A circle illuminates with love the face of the free earth,
The planetary blue diamond is a blossoming sphere,
Stellar rays are united in cosmic energies,
There is attainment of radiations with starlight
Some guides carrying Joys leave their traces,
The appeased sound of the sea looks inside its image,
A collective of love serene the times to come,
The energetic receptive charges arrive from thoughts,
Ascension tools fill bodies in light,
The crystals are connections with the being and the earth,
The circuit of the healing field is the union with nature,
The seven colors of the rainbow are the reflection of chakras,
The lighting torch maintains eternal youth,
Three dolphins travel in the oceans of radiance,
Nature will align and heal all frequencies,
A desert island enjoys the oasis of the clean landscape,
Rebirth to change lives without attaching to anything,
The wheel of existence turns endlessly in the universe,
The majestic polar bear does not need man,
The white ice prepares to be the blue ocean,
Birds roam the skies in search of serenity,
The little birds sing sharing their melodies,
The leaves of trees are the healing of the inner soul,
In the rain seeds die to be born as trees,
The enchanted mountains receive the golden eagle,
The seasons change and without complaining lives spring up,
The sun and the moon look at each other and with their hugs they
love each other,
Within all two wolves struggle to find food,
In survival the most fed will show the destiny.

121 Bilderberg Club

The design of the economic temple has the goal of collapsing,
Offering a plate of food they forget citizen worlds,
Big brother is a lamb in wolf's clothing,
Kindness a la carte with great poisoned intentions,
The satanic order only visualizes a single idea in rules,
The owners of money decide when a crisis ends,
Masonic nights dictate the lesson in silent wars,
The Ten Commandments are the new religion of greed,
The identity cells will be used in tax records,
External memory is already demolishing biology,
The fourth revolution is already here chasing victimhood,
Riddles have more restrictions for freedom,
CRISPR technology searching for virtual humans,
Future happiness passes first through the amount of pleasure,
Feelings will become science fiction between families,
A new programmed human robotic society is born,
The degradation of the human positioned at the level of the object,
Between robots, animals and humans their condition is the same,
Entering perfectionism, euthanasia is an abyss,
The impulse to paradise raises the catastrophe of the mighty,
Academic conferences no longer measure skulls,
The great synthetic reset applies the science that transforms,
The climate crisis will hit the world economy,
The people pulling the trigger agree to be drowned,
Predatory capitalism clothes itself with salvation,
From the top the herd is observed as the plague of the system,
A withering attack is prepared in the club of secrets,
The new accepted models have restricted steps,
The tyrant God Amadeus is fanciful in virtual laughter.

122 The Intruder Law

Health protection among tempting promises,
Peoples trapped under the claws of panthers,
Invading Politician Kidnapped By The Dragon Elite,
Technology no longer requires religious scriptures,
The revolution of the industry has the fusion of the mixture,
The digital introduction draws attention to the cyborg life,
Dominion slowly bombs the addictive screen,
The open territory has been trained for decades,
Discrimination is punished and vaccines are imposed,
Naturalize what is natural but not visible as normal,
Nature is going to be subjected to technological application,
Reconfigure humanity for a start without contamination,
The human species is in the process of reconfiguring itself,
Artificial intelligence picks up the intuitive capabilities,
The rebirth of the process leads to powerful decisions,
The multiplication of content raises the tension to danger,
Responsibilities jump the branches of recognition,
In ambition without dignity the symmetry of power is corruption,
The yoke begins with impositions to destroy humans,
Legislators allow experiments with humanism,
Mutant dystopia in species raises its footprints,
In sentences and defeats the feelings are lost,
On trembling pillars disappointments slide,
The resistant memories between fights wander in their days,
Money buys power where greed fails,
A delirious legacy searches for the trade mark,
Gods compete with the night for not enjoying the day,
Remembering the human being remains in written pages,
The story is critical but the foundations sit unhurriedly.

123 Appearance that Protects

Hidden caves welcome lunatic encounters,
Eternal complaints reflected in infinite and slow defeats,
The distractions of the ego carry loads without determination,
A labyrinth creates sequels between covered networks,
The Martians have landed since centuries ago,
In hidden lodges underground contacts shake hands,
Hellfires catch children from orphanages,
The black nobility chooses the wall of guides in espionage,
The offering caves satanically feed,
The grades rise with the worst ceremonies,
The yoke of Christianity continues to kneel cunningly,
The elite converts the background with language of protection,
The people persecute the limit submerged in false freedom,
Expressions are collected with newscasts of appearances,
The construction of values falls for accepting approvals,
The instrumentalists of the human becomes a subject,
The apparent protector uses people as objects,
Arbitration lands put communities in threats,
Starting the experiment will modify the outputs,
Quacks are not ashamed of criticism,
Epidemics await peoples who sell their liberation,
The magician's vaccine runs to save the beggars,
A code marks the slaves surrounding the identity,
Someone shakes the hornet's nest to attract fear,
Social networks continue to cut the cake in their favor,
The regulation of the system is born from accepting what is prohibited,
Groups meet with hopes of few solutions,
Alone you will not be anyone but with the union the sum is powerful,
Portals are open where knowledge is logic.

124 Become Your Creator

A few words of paper in decisions are accountable,
Morality does not reach Santos, only to recognize itself is to rewrite itself,
The spirit is extinguished in corners of imposed obedience,
When you feel the end of fighting, a beginning will begin
Women are books and men are readers,
The tragedy of life is to become wise too late,
Forgiveness is in the same measure of which you hate,
Books are cold friends but I walk safely
He who cannot give anything is becausehe cannot feel anything,
Elegance is not in fashion but in feeling,
Opinion on earth causes more trouble than earthquakes,
When the devil is satisfied he appears to be a good person,
The one who least needs tomorrow advances towards it,
We all leave life as when we were just born.
You rarely think about what you have, but if you think about what is missing,
Saying I don't have time is the same as saying I don't want to.
When you believe in yourself you don't need to convince anyone.
Perfection is the will to be imperfect,
Difficulties mastered are opportunities gained,
We make a living with what we obtain and we make it with what is offered,
If we open a dispute between past and present, we lose the future,
Charity is not the correct cure for poverty,
You don't know what you know until you teach it to others,
Success is getting up from failures without losing enthusiasm,
Courage uses ingenuity to cross the adventure of the sea,
The one who shares and distributes keeps the best part,
Each person is the owner of his silence and slave of his word,
Being loved by someone gives you strength, loving someone gives you courage,
He who excuses himself is accused.

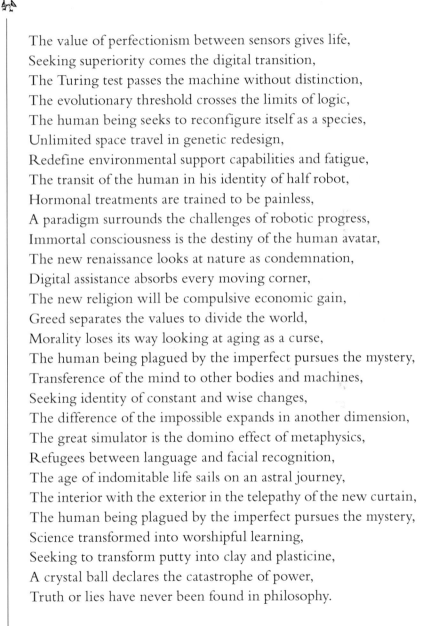

125 Transhumanism

The value of perfectionism between sensors gives life,
Seeking superiority comes the digital transition,
The Turing test passes the machine without distinction,
The evolutionary threshold crosses the limits of logic,
The human being seeks to reconfigure itself as a species,
Unlimited space travel in genetic redesign,
Redefine environmental support capabilities and fatigue,
The transit of the human in his identity of half robot,
Hormonal treatments are trained to be painless,
A paradigm surrounds the challenges of robotic progress,
Immortal consciousness is the destiny of the human avatar,
The new renaissance looks at nature as condemnation,
Digital assistance absorbs every moving corner,
The new religion will be compulsive economic gain,
Greed separates the values to divide the world,
Morality loses its way looking at aging as a curse,
The human being plagued by the imperfect pursues the mystery,
Transference of the mind to other bodies and machines,
Seeking identity of constant and wise changes,
The difference of the impossible expands in another dimension,
The great simulator is the domino effect of metaphysics,
Refugees between language and facial recognition,
The age of indomitable life sails on an astral journey,
The interior with the exterior in the telepathy of the new curtain,
The human being plagued by the imperfect pursues the mystery,
Science transformed into worshipful learning,
Seeking to transform putty into clay and plasticine,
A crystal ball declares the catastrophe of power,
Truth or lies have never been found in philosophy.

A black swan conspires between force and justice,
Civilization collapses due to the dominance of delusion,
The human destined to be an object for experiments,
Microchips will be the gatekeepers in pursuit,
Restrictions for food consumption with bonus,
The deteriorating economy is concentrated in a crypto currency,
Constant vigilance will not allow decisions to be made,
Promising offers to start sterilization,
Proposals for surrogacy for in vitro fertility,
The cybernetic doctrine will be the greatest family bond,
The volunteers of the system will be the young generation,
The low rainbow without colors in the land of science,
Theoretical developments will fix a centrist religion,
Feeding on natural products from marginalized countries,
Hunger oppression will bring acceptance of resources,
The backpack of victims seeks to be filled to be acclaimed,
The defender chooses the problem to be chosen powerful,
The racial world imposes itself as the theory of order,
Irresponsible minds accuse themselves to offer him salvation,
The theory is to accuse peoples of being polluters,
The perfect storm is to oppress damaging feelings,
Pointing out to the submissive how savage the herd applauds,
From the horizon the piper is enchanting the lost,
The government promises paradise with enchanted tales,
The obedience monopoly has a domino effect,
When dark footsteps are perceived, some waves rebel,
Police assistance is on every corner with dominance,
Dreams turn into sewer profits,
Humans in the exhausting world kneel.

127 Day Zero

The water counts the days with the begging winds,
The wind dreams in nights of hidden nightmares,
Life becomes cloudy and leaves lost what was left behind,
On the blurred road an old forgotten wound is born,
People get strange pretending to fly,
They can't cry in need, just look for courage,
Amnesia of the partial moment is an eclipse in anxiety,
Uncontrolled pollution devours the ocean,
The main supply of life is covered with bitterness,
A town with chemical battles are cannon fodder,
Pioneering mistakes repeat waiting for the big crater,
The volcano will swallow the obedient herd of the system,
A nest is reserved for the navigators of power,
Noiselessly towers rise to make separations,
The road is a whip where the ashes leave burns,
No need to try to blow where greed took hold,
The one who wanted to love put rules against the current,
The lack of reasoning imposes the doses with measures,
The outbreak of claims raises news but no changes,
The commandments are imposed to terrorize society,
Poverty chains freedom in not making decisions,
The tables of the law break the harmony between coexistence,
The cave of the dragon puts the concentration camp to sleep,
War can kill once but politics a thousand times.
Garbage dumped in oceans will come back with a rage,
The zero day does not know the limited temporary space,
There is no change of the past that teaches,
There is only a new beginning from the beginning.

128 Metaverse

The goal from the earth in a universal garden walk,
Hunting in the virtual reality is wrapped in natural,
A twin world leaps into the digitized dimension,
A teleport journey offering a new century,
Virtual dating is here to stay in holograms,
The avatars will be the inseparable companions, 3D glasses, more
than living in reality, are also felt,
A new step raises the fuel of real time,
A great attraction unites the ceremoniesin a theater,
The virtual concert unites minds but not hearts,
The era of physical solitude connected to the united world,
Between parallel lives the companion avatar is chosen,
Intense emotions travel with selected cartoons,
The universal walks changing sadness of moments,
Weather Navigator relaxes visual screens,
Chained innovation in the business world,
The virtual city lives and breathes like the physical city,
The content of the essential is linked to reality,
The metaverse district is the future surveillance key,
Contemplation of hope in the future of the challenge,
The development of the celebration running for happiness,
The prohibitions of ignorance seeking wisdom,
Such devastating beauty penetrates in an eclipse,
The life of the unequal designing the science of separation,
The blind sadness emptying the humility in the bonfire,
The Lost Body in Imprisoned Voluntary Simulations,
The crisis of love tied to a mask of lonely power,
Some challenges are a comedy among many questions.

129 The Pill of Choice

Dictators go in a direction with submission to what is foreign,
The operating tech giants sound between bursts,
The machine of the new order is introduced to the confrontation,
Challenges and restrictions bring mediocre alternatives,
Minds are pigeonholed into complex dubious cultures,
Conservatism is insufficient for liberation,
Threats of speech surround the four corners,
Worship is more goal-oriented than union,
The challenges present the company of skills,
Separating faith from reason, consolation accompanies,
An experiment can be the decision of the new beginning,
Any sneeze is good to put your head down,
The red mirror of the dragon is close to new frontiers,
The prize in a sentence is the temptation of consumption,
There is cruelty feigning kindness between black and white,
Strange burrows drag shadows that haunt us,
The lack of historical vision takes away the beauty of life,
In an open cage it is impossible to escape from mortality,
Something sublime surrounds the landscape but fear hides it,
Philosophy hopes to fill the void with maturity,
Efforts consuming the health of many like fire,
Challenges arrogated to the world in a treacherous journey,
Dangerous sailors in search of new worlds,
Star conquests hoping to see closer,
When looking at the ground, the ancestors leave traces of food,
The dare to dream leaves the harmonica playing,
The beauty of the world reflecting dreams of light and darkness,
Between danger and comfort lies madness and lucidity.
The environment layouts force you to choose the pill.

130 Stories on Paper

A canned plan has the world in a paper doll
The reality is harsh where methods promise liberation,
The darts meeting invades the election target,
Fear goes hand in hand with the fellowship of the slave,
Ruled by science and reason, they seek a happy world,
Creating the normal, the other side of the coin is visualized,
Objects are designed and identity is dehumanized,
Comfort is selected by capacity,
The guides provide offers in exchange for removing powers,
Clone armies are trustworthy mutants,
A technical world sails towards a controlled state,
A lost paradise has already separated the sea from the land,
The heart of heaven watches without being able to look back,
The instrument of gods risks the expired calendar,
The sands of time leave splendid beats,
Looking for a better world is like a dish ordered a la carte,
Education and respect is the basis of primordial development,
The moral compass visualizes a course to be defined,
Horror breaks out and frivolity only watches screens,
Distraction with diplomacy befriends fraud,
Education needs workers trained to obey,
The calm in the midst of the storm is an obligatory veil,
The society of desire does not bring satisfaction of success,
When the addicted mind calms down, frustration devours,
The hero's agony turns his mirror in search of triumphs,
The horizon offers something synthetic to replicate the origin,
Illusion and science happens in unpredictable variations,
Immersed in the artificial what can be measured is effectiveness,
The art of being happy becomes an amazing journey.

The Miserables

The soul flees and surrenders between triumph and despair,
A piece of bread can catch goodness in a sentence,
Medieval lines make destinations trapped in deserts,
A miserable world kneels divine salvation,
The horizon of poverty separates love with struggles,
Monarch systems between tyrannies make blind eyes,
The memory hides with an empty background,
The searches become distances with constant obstacles,
Innocence feels the shadow that pursues freedom,
Hope sows a work transformed nights and days,
The laughs are sad, between delays, disturbing exits,
Each breath becomes a sigh between the guilt of living,
Tempting fruits fall that are gathered for salvation,
Prayers become reflections with doubts,
A few lines of ink melt with silent tears,
The sweetness of memory welcomes an embrace of splendor,
A swan flies in dreams to calm bitterness,
Every moment becomes a labyrinthine race,
The last moment seems like a tunnel closer and further away,
In deep wounds the cold hands reach out to the voice,
Cruel whispers leave traces of secrets with effort,
The corners are like claws to rest from nightmares,
The look hides between passageways that devour,
The critics are spies with the hidden face of crime,
An impulsive passenger between coins points to victims,
Running in madness ashes of loneliness are beating,
The heart has the flame lit from the belly,
They blow stubborn complaints and inside they burn,
The absence of consolation acclaims the spirit in death.

132 Shortage

A mutation spreads from digital networks,
Between clothes and food come the decisions of fear,
Between books and medicines,
Health or education sighs,
The threshold of control manipulates masses in slavery and mind,
The taxes suffocate and with the escapes they suffocate,
The little there is between the ignorancethat devours,
The aid funds do not have economic capacity,
Disasters have been knocking on the door for decades,
The guardians no longer distribute the water to survive,
Divisions create suicidal towns with a dead stop,
Wages are consumed in the food increase,
Primordial velocity loses oxygen between slits,
The steps are made thought of in panic and disappointment,
Inequality carries tsunamis in punishing glances,
An elevator is very full and on the way up it got stuck,
The engine of the economy has an irreparable fissure,
The correction machine was imprisoned in two axes,
Offer keys are injected to shelter the wolf,
One wave appears to be protective, another engulfs the middle class,
The riots seek an index to start over,
Artificial intelligence begins to be the boss of crazy people,
The filters are already sealed so as not to return to the past,
An accelerator separates borders into needs,
A formula creates infected vitamins in cages without exits
Symptoms become soothing but not curative,
The cracks of the explosive growl in the time bomb,
An accelerator appears and turns the world in the other direction,
A machine arrives and triggers inflation with universal collapse,
We are servants of the system for a world that does not exist.

133 World Where are You Going?

The dimensions approach accompaniedby the avatar,
The future is accelerated in constant learning surprises,
The mutant ecosystem leaves behind the old generation,
Universal wisdom grows with causes and motives,
The rules bring capacity where connections begin,
Changes travel seeking their own place of knowledge,
The sandwich and qualified generation has many questions,
The thought of seeking help is an analysis that paralyzes,
Values are tools created from responses,
Contracts are key from the independent potential,
Rebirth is in development to crack the game,
The robotic race leads the seated traveler,
The conquering limits transform political history,
A frontal and expert shock replaces the human system,
The biblical disaster breaks in the bubble of confrontation,
The restart of growth is the inertia of progress,
Synthetic vigilance is formed with unstoppable abilities,
The future already conquers consciousness with the digital age,
In reality you own nothing and own everything,
A dizzying storm destroys compulsive consumption,
The challenges between the games seem like unattainable challenges,
In battles, conquests entail a great effort,
The beginnings open doors to make the falls visible,
An infinite corridor offers dizzying paths of learning,
The old giant loses competition without centralized currencies,
Clarity defeats the power in weapons of darkness,
Time does not remember the identity of the repeated past,
Between the big and the small the earth devours alike,
A guardian world of codes shows silent logic.

134 The Eye Contour

Two wings of the same party fit into a single script,
The leader does not wait for the slave but the slave waits for the leader.
Some creatures are lost in the night of tears,
The infantilized societies seek a pope government,
The mission of wolves is to sacrifice wretches without mercy,
The information economy is the oil of power,
The thought police control crimes of the future,
The society of the spectacle cracks the circus,
Fighting for adventures does not adapt values to limits,
The obedient culture experiences a hallucinogenic empire,
The cage of knowledge makes the herd more prisoner,
The mafia of power adjusts the psychology to the target,
Opus Dei is the best secret driver in adaptations,
Those who fight for God's favor are the least peaceful,
Obligations are announced but deaf ears to humanity,
Bloodline Masons trap volunteers for dominance,
The cults separate families to turn their gear,
The church is more united in destruction than in pastoral,
The demands grow in paradigms of acclamation,
The human on paradise earth is a universal virus,
Running in madness they forget the sound of the waves of the sea,
Solidarity residents navigate in a poisoned society,
A world without existence destroys itself among its guides,
Borders are obstacles in the great foreign world,
The ghosts wander in a traumatized revolution,
On the horizon the system of the beast does not escape the crisis,
A word that escapes the lips will never go back,
The divine voice is hidden from the internal dialogue but will be reborn,
The light that pierced the darkness shattered the glass of fear.

135 Identity

Night falls in a sky without seeing the stars of the universe,
The moon grows cold without the rays of the fellow sun,
The sky of the earth does not have the colors of the rainbow,
The flowers sleep on their petals of reincarnation,
The method of science screams in results for systems,
The battlefield loses its calm between sick and well,
Communication screens are symptoms for aggressiveness,
Between digital antennas the dragon blinks and the wolf howls,
Colonial empires hide the card game,
A global cult envisions the hive's Jake-mate,
Travel has roots in the summits of the world,
By the fruits the tree is known to assess the path,
The lord of darkness flees from love because fear blinds him,
The fugitive can run but can't escape control,
The bonfire became a court of the inquisition,
The internal lion wants to loosen the chains to be able to roar,
The society of the spectacle is a parasite in front of screens,
Paradise in illusion lives an empire of fantasies,
The reflection chases the simulation levels in the mirror,
Between limits of comedies we create a polarized sense,
Demonstrations creating goodness without knowing how to share,
Creators of a false revolution between reason and solution,
Being smart an intellectual fashion looking to be free,
A monster designs how to eliminate the evil of limits,
Society is infantilized in the image of the comment,
In the infinite wait, uncertainty seeks to adapt,
The demands try to correct the temperament,
Race disconnected us, religion separated us, politics divided us.

136 Space Program

The grim fate brings the earth to the collision gate,
The light bodies prepare in telepathic transportation,
Sonic treatments are for communicative expansion,
Secret teachings come from advanced dimensions,
Space travel is separated into ceremonies and cultures,
The spheres offer a potion to sleep in time,
Host bubbles expose bodies in secret,
The frozen giants begin to awaken,
Body snatchers do code swapping,
Spaceships carry impulses with dampers,
Anti-gravity technology provides portal travel,
The life of a thousand years is in the visiting guests,
The asteroid belt marks the footprints of Mars,
A reddish indigenous race envelops the footsteps of Mars,
Burrowing insects continue their course in the territory,
Between the speed of light time changes matter,
Some magnetic bracelets merge between magic,
Parallel contours create realities between past and future,
Secret societies have rooms for clones,
In no man's land old souls are kidnapped,
Astral projection unites the spirit in reptilian souls,
The moon has alien invasions in underground,
Humanoid bases follow agreements contracts,
Lunar commandos seriously keep restrictions,
Reptilian groups use breakthrough control in their caves,
Continental invasions are marked in lodges,
The elite military are dark fleets of chemicals,
Genetic soldiers receive particle injections,
Lunar stations between conferences impose rules.

A window opens where the air passes between currents,
A heavenly fantasy watches the earth glittering,
From a far east a ship visits the starry sea,
A swirling wind raised a ray of light on the water,
The collapsing earth sighs care and attention,
Supplies churn in the pollution caused,
Drinking water is in short supply for life,
The forest jungle is in constant danger mutilation,
The calm in the storm watches the eye of the hurricane,
They seek to roar wonders between dreams without nightmares,
Birds are declining and the human population has doubled,
The pillars of life watch the satellite of evolution,
Star sculpture is more amazing than science,
Living parallel lives the origin will remain a mystery,
A star factory welcomes the birth of planets,
Spiraling an invisible hole awaits,
Inside the horizon is still the galaxy,
Between wonders and dangers the secrets live together,
Fascinating forests with one tree make up the picture,
The crowns of shining dust unite with the universe,
Between distance and closeness, nothing becomes everything,
Between light and darkness energies are fed,
Some diamonds explode where fire is rebirth
In unanswered questions the profound spirit is born,
Siren songs find exits in labyrinths,
A cosmic haystack recalls the orbits between comets,
The dark magical ocean creates embryonic galaxies,
Where the universal waves expand in messages,
The heavenly library illuminates the return of the heart.

The Stellar Invasion

The sowing of humans forms the following slavery,
Consciousness thieves block higher planes,
Star systems have the cosmic web invaded,
Every solar system has portals with transit trips,
The matrix force can imprison the force bear,
Near the apocalypse the sky of the chronic earth will fall,
Mind control is the key to progress in submission,
Dehumanized values enslave themselves,
The distant horizons are fed with other energies,
The eye of the volcano keeps holograms in the silence,
Galactic authority competes for interstellar power,
Travelers form colonies in solar systems,
The guardians of technology are the gray aliens,
A whirlpool of time spreads out in regressions,
A dark abyss erases the Martian background,
Color borders in new space worlds,
Between the end times is the farewell to the world,
Wandering planets dance around asteroids,
Among the dangers await undiscoveredwonders,
The cosmic chimneys in their roars are raging,
Embraces of icy rocks are tears of darkness,
More spheres of the limitless universe sail in the cosmos,
Voyages to infinity seek unbaptized worlds,
A star bottle guides a map with thousands of languages,
The heavenly machine is a small ant step,
Interstellar space has no direction of end or beginning,
An acceleration of stars attracts the hidden worlds,
Challenges remind us that we are like sand,
A hypnotic jellyfish surrounded by the universe of gods.

A lonely stage drawn to Saturn's belt,
The six-faced storms between photogenic beauty light,
The particles of ceremonies in their adventure rings,
The planet of the seven wonders gives magical moons,
The bubble skies between streams with methane rain,
A sheltered moon accompanies gaseous and cold lakes,
Between fugitive colors magical landscapes are visualized,
Some lost rings plunge into deep oceans,
Between guides and spirits something is wrapped terrifying and
beautiful,
A step towards the light is gestated in the near future,
A circle in the shadows reflect entities and ghosts,
A faint whisper holds the skies of remembrance,
Flying on the futuristic satellite is like swimming in the ocean,
The beats of the wind wrap the lakes in songs,
The guide of planets wrapped in a ring of asteroids,
The navigation of a dream between enigmatic moons,
An adventure surrounds the renaissance of space art,
A boy hugging the solar system park,
A majestic float attracts masses in attractive colors,
A spiral enters a journey of regressive galaxies,
A snowflake dances through the magic orbit,
The cosmic ballet inverts its hemispheres with brilliance,
The dimensions greet the curtains of traveling smoke,
Oceans and continents in the dark envelop landscapes,
An alien world hides sleeping gardens,
Some golden rocks flow with sound on the surface,
Dreams enter the shores of dim worlds,
The splendor of engineering delivers brighter challenges,
The mysteries collide opening unlimited universes.

140 Martian City

The great planetary suicide is prepared for combat,
The two moons of Mars connecting with Teotihuacan,
Sound signals greet the robotic drones,
In the night of time a capsule is life,
Mount Olympius spits lava from the ancient volcano,
Between its great canyon a crack opens long paths,
Radioactive wind storms show their fury,
The energetic cold shows the hidden face of fire,
The protective union Goddess Nüwa becomes a refuge,
The gem of infinity carves its ore in emerald beauty,
The red cliff opens a solar temple in digital security,
The electronic police is constantly monitored,
Robotic surveillance is the reign of regulatory order,
The new generation shares the lost values,
Living in community is a compulsory cliff,
Insects become food delicacy,
The next frontier of the red planet will be respect,
The detectives on Mars will be the humanoid robots,
The volcanic province Elysium is the spa resort of the oasis,
In the land of pearls an artificial climate will open a paradise,
The deserted snow cracks will open ski slopes,
Between dry rivers and dunes gear canals are born,
The sad pages close with new opportunities,
The mistakes of the past are chained to evictions,
The domes are tuned between military rulers,
Imperial records have severe restrictions,
Biocatalysts control human reproduction,
Birth policies are watched with caution,
The valleys wait to be reborn in terrestrial memories,
The great filter of life approaches another arrow of time.

141   Moon Base

Celestial bodies explore with jumps in zero gravity,
A few trips of rain of stars dance in the galaxy,
The city without borders opens doors and windows,
Between challenges the lunar dust accompanies a thousand dangers,
In its cold magnetism it is bombarded by meteorites,
In its dull image, its inner brightness is a splendor,
In his voice of blows the sounds flow in songs,
The sublime star of eclipse with transshipment to the universe,
From its sublime sphere minerals shine in sparkles,
Between swirling storms cosmic rays greet,
From distant gazes mysterious gods acclaim him,
Property of poets dreamers in pages mark their mark,
Sovereign sea of tranquility in the white nights,
The hidden face is silent in the shining dark,
Behind science a ring of light orbits rebirth,
Within the magical and mysterious treasures are hidden,
The conquering moon is watched by the stars,
The master sorcerer sun with its rays illuminates him,
Some afternoons with bright eyes attracted white smiles,
In its silent turns remember that life is an instant,
Cold arid lagoons run through the memories of lagoons,
Night of hidden treasure under rocks flows its cold water,
As a child who begins to live sees everything in colors,
The guides bind the ties on galactic horizons,
Challenges remind us that we are all like sand,
Like a hypnotic jellyfish that surrounds the transparent sea,
Trying to be gods we forget to enjoy life,
The great lady of the night in the vicinity unites distances,
The great dance partner of the beautiful earth family.

142 Space Hotel

A new era dawns in planetary conquest,
A space cruise around the wondrous earth,
The invisible generation surrounds the traveler with separation,
Conquering the universe with the tourists of the future,
Without warnings or plans, the androidsaccompany smiles,
Futuristic Noah's ark opens glass case with fate,
The majestic odyssey bubble without mountains or hills,
The sun lights up comets at the end of nights and days,
The celestial asteroids walk in their currents,
Meteor shower shimmers in stellar arenas,
The cosmic dust traveling between the terrestrial sky,
A fan of dreams focuses the beating of telescopes,
The technology of infinity delivered to the universe is woven,
In footprints and systems, space traffic greets terrestrial traffic,
Space time will host a new interstellar human,
The illusion becomes the moment of light and darkness,
A journey of mystery surrounds the limits of floating seas,
In the smallest image the fierce movement surrounds us,
Traveling the infinite distance light years are theories,
Some unknown island from beyond watches,
Songs of northern lights illuminate the solar system,
The expansion of the universe paints enigmas of harmony,
The breath of the whole between cells of the celestial dragon,
The dream with the awakening unites a desert of peace,
Between monsters and angels the storm meets,
A plunge into hypnosis recalls the miracle of life,
The circle of a star with the supreme doctrine,
The dimensional teaching between spheres of the spirit,
A spark in glory leaves a thousand questions unanswered.

143 Embracing Silence

In an accelerated time, thought seeks calm,
Swinging in harmony a light finds laughter,
The best answers are found between forgetting,
In unabashed thoughts the best ideas arise,
By uniting songs in silence, rebirth is cultivated,
Meditation strengthens the creativity of the soul,
The density of the interior creates more folds in wisdom,
Delicious slowness manages the world of speed,
The fast-paced world needs a brake on speed,
Haste is a virus in the journey of the addicted generation,
The language of the goal is the creation of less is more,
A lumberjack slows down the conquest of green forests,
A filter seeks the reflection between the wise nature,
To embrace reconquests is to act slowly in silence,
The dinner of the disciples is a magical effect of union,
The social skill is the development of balance,
A shared puzzle comes together with slow pleasure,
A visualized ritual is creation of human touch,
The best sanctuary crosses few words with silences,
Between floods the moon cleanses the sky of the exhausted sea,
Together in solitude art is shared in thought,
The encounter with oneself is a cornerstone,
In the metaphysics of union the tasks leave metamorphosis,
Make learning more important than grades,
Make sport an entertainment not a competition,
Pauses in races make brilliant athletes,
Calming cults of challenges the paths are opening,
Open the door to a ladybug where looks play,
The mind controls the body but the breath controlled it.

Great actions start from small progress,
Playing to find an identity we become objects,
An avalanche of dreams turns into nightmares,
Seeking to choose with measures and separating the deteriorated,
The triumph of infinity disturbs the worker ants,
Force becomes condemnation in the callof power,
The dark tyrants drag the present in a blackout,
Manipulation generates an infantilized society,
The world is run by the race of the mightiest,
The value of reason seems to be buried in the past,
The cynical society keeps spinning in endless questions,
Science and technology advances more than understanding,
An electric sheep is created with a language of effects,
Where the facts pass, words pass before,
Some lines cross evil in processes of discriminating,
Fragile reality raises walls but keeps crying,
Rules appear union with limits that mark holes,
The wisdom of ignorance seizes greatness from humble,
An equation of numbers vibrates between forgetting and remembering,
In the intelligent abyss is found the most artificial,
Models in successes with doubts about democratic identity,
Sinister theories in constant vows of existence,
A watch stands amongst a brutal history of turbulence,
A competition between clashes with invasion to defeats,
Sinister democracies darken in pride,
A cold war arena counts the limits in defiance,
A lightning bolt drops its tears of reflection,
A short existence is the lesson that pain seizes,
Predicting the impossible is not created only conquered.

145 Magical Society

Following the footsteps of the past leads to the cliff,
Large businesses say goodbye to digital,
A handle of opportunities turns dreams into desires,
The challenges continue in virtual reality and crucially,
The free individual loses in choices of consumerism,
Obligations condemn with efforts of responsibility,
The society of tiredness makes distant people,
Enlarge the positive for the system that smiles or dies,
The fight against depression is overcome with difficulty,
The hidden side gear doesn't trust the outside,
A superficial world with an interior of observer and observed,
The money ethic is the fantasy of identity and progress,
The crisis becomes the mighty big brother,
Loneliness brings an emptiness of coldness in the union of love,
Tales and legends are customs in the new apocalypse,
In the face of lies, the rules go further than the truth,
The wars of the future are the keys to generating abundance,
Raised for a world where respect no longer exists,
A dark hope leaves fate in chancellor's test,
Without a fixed course we look for culprits to continue the separation,
Embracing prosperity, the transit of the leader is acclaimed,
The illusion of time rests in a social tomb,
The loyalty of pleasure is replaced with unfeeling machines,
A world of black humor overcomes difficult barriers,
A sunken labyrinth creates the avatar to survive,
With the genre of science the future seems to fly,
The intelligence numbers look for keys of changes,
The miraculous frequency awaits evolutionary maturity,
The crazy history of mankind is under constant surveillance.

146 Purification

An invisible journey meditates on the comedy of hope,
A map replaces the territory with an authoritarian cycle,
The human chain modified to the condition of the program.
Factory of obedient citizens turned into numbers,
The assembly of chains is a system applied by hierarchies,
A mechanical content applied to the order of the program,
A light goes out in the silence to look elsewhere,
When the blow of fate brings man to his knees,
The straps of tears are released to see a sigh,
Reborn from the unconscious by conscious forgetting,
In laughter are the rays of the sun united with the moon and stars,
Peace are pillars that supported the earth and the sky,
We know the price of everything but with the value of nothing,
By abandoning the ego, the miracles of the encounter begin,
When you embrace loneliness you will feel the conquest,
The beginning and the end is the beauty of eternity,
What can the man who lives between the sun and the moon say?
Between gods and beasts the written stories are mixed,
Delivered hope mixed with bitterness,
By not following anyone then like a fish you are free,
Identity is the encounter with thought and emotion,
Humanity finds itself on an orphan path,
The hope of nothingness goes blank before flashes,
After denial comes anger with pacts,
A person aware of love is not a predator,
You cannot subdue a river, you have to surrender to it,
Using the current in favor is like flying to infinity,
Peace is the best poem that is remodeling everything.

147 Between Fleet Water

The origin of the galaxy shares the notes of the universe,
A fire sows brilliance to the beat of a flutist,
An indomitable crocodile dives among meadows,
In the deep ocean the skin of the sea welcomes the rivers,
Its agitated currents greet the caresses of the wind,
The children of the sun without borders live a brave dream,
In the wild and the sweet the heart beats with attraction,
The tropical waters like mirrors enchant the sky,
Calm Magic moves the wand of the united spirit,
The circle of secrets adorns the earth with gaps,
Mountain waterfalls shed happy tears,
The enchantment of stars travels in the fleeting nature,
Some plants float sailing in freedom of procreation,
It is the dance of the planet that shapes the floating navigation,
The islands anchor the waves in sonorous peaceful waves,
Between eddies a desert turns into snow,
A kind face shows its enemy side of time,
A cocktail of monsters and gods fly in secret,
Predators in heavenly skies howl between volcanoes,
The springs welcome wild birds of the kingdom,
The colors of the glittering sea are copies of its inhabitants,
Where the valleys of ravens cry out with melodies,
Lady's shoes paint their flowers in silence,
In tropical jungles belongs the illusion of treasures,
Mantra chants hail forest protection,
The corner of emeralds guards her heavenly lungs,
The colored trails offer a home for animals,
The mysterious anaconda queen reminds that life is fleeting,
Where the battle of the universe is a shamanic music.

148 A Flower in The Desert

The sky remains the last frontier of destiny.
A small talisman illuminates the dreams of each one,
Discovering the value the look attracts support and benefits,
Intuition has no borders or questions or answers,
It is the open air that wraps the tree in each day,
Where passion accompanies the spirit envelops the rhythm,
The pilgrim without a compass marks his footprints in destiny,
Each thought accompanies the tireless whirlpool,
Nature accompanies the songbird of flight,
The mountain greets the stars from closer,
The streams travel paths where the wind guides them,
The seas speak with the waves where the sun looks at the moon,
Butterflies dance in the breeze and flowers sparkle,
Soft jasmine reveals submerging with aromas,
Between laughter and tears the moon lights up in dreams,
A hunter of time drops a tear on stone,
Some shifting dunes hide their trail in the sand,
Bright eyes look across borders,
An oasis of waves leaves pebbles between yellow lines,
Thorns of immense cacti look at the shining sun,
A nomadic paradise is wrapped in the mirror of the wind,
A shimmering road veils the silence,
A mysterious face keeps in longed for hope,
Eternity teaches the art of infinite mystery,
Imagination creates the fertile reality in the lost choir,
Where the invented punishment implores forgiveness on its knees,
While gold and silver respect their white hills,
Energy is a treasure accompanied by the life star,
A flower in the desert opens a tunnel to the oasis of paradise.

149 Cryogenized People

Humans hibernating while science awakens,
Slowing down the biological clock sleeps minds and cells,
A hologram suits in cybernetic mortality,
Nano rehabilitation proceeds to brain clones,
A primate lethargy passes in robotic phase of control,
Rising dead is the futuristic genetics of the universe,
Distant cities double the oxygen of survival,
The evolution of a thousand years traveling in space time,
A deep alien sleep plunges into the abyss,
A present with a past falls into a hole of hope,
Regression tells the moon of ages past,
Bridges trigger memories from ties on hold,
The changes are a journey between other worlds,
Quantum limits adapt the reality of the journey,
Adaptation intersects with the laws of chemistry,
Alchemy becomes a real work of fiction,
Rising from the hole the day begins to emerge,
As morning falls, the next modified existence arrives,
Virtual souls sail in the spirit of a spiral,
Between synthetic energies power expands technology,
Microchips are the constellations of paradise,
The androids blend the sound into the golden silence,
Immortality looks at the sky with the illusion of being reborn,
The colors are involved in a game without limits,
A double explosion is in the hands of masters,
A magic pill enters the dream of the return,
An embrace of the tsunami wraps the shadow in divine light,
History conquers kingdoms in art engineering,
Illusion calms the mind in the darkness of islands.

Battle of The Future

Capitalism without measures injects private property,
Living hidden in science manipulated societies,
A mechanism that satisfies the need with limits,
Competition dominates marking economic crises,
The keys convert offers into limited demands,
Social inequality allows stepping on challenges,
Freedom of rights becomes a challenge to disaster,
House arrests become a target,
Accustoming the population to obedience is the continuation,
Social training will be the excuse for a better future,
Emergency alchemy in the hands of psychosis,
The hands of control in a fight of madness,
The global digital power is destined to control,
The modern electronic age drags the mission of sin,
Planetary debt traps the elite in punishing decisions,
The change of course seeks a new trans humanism,
An ancient model collapses on the dark tunnel route,
Narcissism expands between punishing debts,
The identity in the crisis wants excuses not to think,
The achievements between traps bring invisible nostalgia,
Looking for happiness, you forget to build the road, capricious
humanity seeks reasons to feel,
The abyss of loneliness lies around the next corner,
Exceeding the limits ends in more economic demands,
Consumerism is the prize that fills the gaps,
A chaos of explosions consumes the energy in errors,
Fear seeks constant threats to calm,
Civilization preserves the consciousness of the empire,
The norms determine the black nobility of the temple.

151 A Hidden Side

Health is the enthusiasm of the magicalside to live,
Obstacles are opportunities to measure your limits,
Learn to unlearn to face fanaticism,
The balance is focused on the connection of the whole,
What is not practiced is forgotten, withering in ashes,
The talent of the heart opens mysterious values,
The paradox of the sky enters the desert kingdom,
When there is something better in each day, old age does not persecute you,
Embracing compatibility talents develop,
The frequency of happiness is the melody of living in peace,
The effort breaks the chain of the dancer in a dance,
The seed remembers that when you are ready the teacher appears,
Sometimes you are lost but in the silence you find yourself,
The road is an infinite plan to fill it in eternity,
Training is willpower that breaks down walls,
In contemplation the structure of an idea is created,
Indecision is the thief of pleasure and opportunities,
To shine look to the past forgiving and thanking,
A teacher understands the child to channel his teaching,
Competition is a trip that paralyzes growth,
The questions of a child are the wonders of philosophy,
The best ceremonies are the essence of good dialogues,
Children are the mirror of the present without hours or agendas,
Success is a journey not a destination to follow the rules,
Getting on the train of changes makes us flexible to progress,
The intention is the origin of everything and the action creates miracles,
The world is full of forgotten treasure maps,
The best travel notebook is to never stop learning,
The beautiful story of your life acts from within.

The North Pole looks at the South Pole from the shooting stars,
Feelings are connected with reckless levels,
Telepathy is part of what envelops the clouds,
Travelers know each other but forget in memories,
The seed is born from nothing and becomes everything,
In the desert a train passes where few tourists get off,
The watching passengers ask when they will return,
Among so many people each one is a grain of sand,
Each city stirs in so many separate cultures,
Something empty and full at the same time confuses trust,
The clock counts down the minutes while waiting to move,
Some silences break the sound of rocky rivers,
Sad smiles await the notes of some song,
The owner of happiness is not always a source of Joy,
Life is like a mirror between hidden results,
The key of smiles fits in everyone's heart,
The Child recognizes the mother by the smile of love,
Sadness is a disease worse than bacteria
Humble joy shines brighter than golden sadness,
Happiness is appreciated from sadness in silence,
There are scars that cry without shedding a tear,
The deceptions are the distraction to believe to be free,
By healing the fear you return to the home of the inner garden,
The journey of time discovers destiny crying and laughing,
The invisible silence shows the way to rest,
Difficult situations like a waterfall reach the sea,
Where a tear reflects a bird flies again,
The colors of nature are the smile of the universe,
Smile and happiness have the same world language.

153 The Masters of The World

These are strange times in a carousel of appearances,
The face towards reality is like an instrument of power,
Remaining attentive traps us in forgetting to live in the present,
By being drawn regulations the next continues,
The classified borders are separated into three crisis blocks,
Glass is brittle in contrast to fuzzy glass,
Crusader comparable perish under the Russian ice,
A warren puts choices between new inventories,
Intentions move the chips at opportunistic levels,
The renaissance of piracy enters the mental union,
The key piece is the following theory that enslaves the will,
Implementations are offers without tuning opportunities,
Microchip graphics keep waves of obedience,
The challenges become energy transportation,
The clones are intentional in search of immortality,
The avatars of the system are the substitutes in security,
From an armchair, life makes the sound of desire,
The chosen choices are reflected with the objective of control,
In the streams of science experiments kill in discreet,
Artificial intelligence is surpassing its creators,
The nuclear winter where drought defies the climate,
Pandemic bioengineering is the suicide strategy,
Secret meetings are created with system prestige,
Dominance points the way to world progress,
Authoritarian ceremonies seek to modify humanity,
The government of the shadow between the doors of luxury hotels,
The threads of power entangle the crises of capitalism,
The modified plans are stealing the dreams,
The silence of the sky keeps a circle of secret echoes.

154 Mental Control

The rules become religions forced to care,
The mechanisms of the game look towards a global objective,
In an alliance of dominance the practice materializes,
The core of lineages is designed with the same scenario,
Few hands emerge in the groups of themovement,
The news that silences is directed with visualization,
Enemy fire arises in the shadow of borders,
Annual selections meet innocents,
Ideologies wear discreet filters with discipline,
The society of the system only keeps distracted traces,
The distance of the system separates the interior from the exterior,
The wars movement rises as business treasure
Education is the science of control from analysis
The elite of the lodge have restricted doors in the temple,
The heirs leave the people submerged in submission,
Freedom peeks out from the distance of loneliness,
An Arab spring awaits economic disaster,
The tyrant continues to offer protection in chess,
The vulnerable people are among deceptions,
The cyberterrorists are a board of the stalked Jake,
Dangerous parasites are feeding on society,
Using the trauma in beliefs, puppets are formed,
The victims of the herd are led without resistance,
Among the powerful, the non-essentials lose security,
Normality becomes regulatory traps,
Manipulation declares the useless as disability,
Shadow churches are members of mind control,
Isolation is the governing norm for an interest,
Between placid dreams storms steal children's destinies.

Adrift world in a comfortable ship of necessities,
We elect arrogant leaders to become opinions,
Only who sees the strings can handle them in power,
Using heaven and hell divide the elections,
The system uses silent weapons for quiet wars,
Selling responsibilities we lose the revolution,
The empire of fantasies is sickened by cultural battle,
Uncertainty is terrified by the encounter with the union,
Loving what does not exist avoids getting involved in commitments,
Everything similar to normal are just created norms,
The best existence is the balance of extended thought,
Good against bad inventing a frequency of light,
A great fight awaits to rise from the newbattle,
An artificial nature adapted the myth of origins,
Ideas of truth have no chemical evidence,
The way of life depends on death to survive,
The order interprets reality in order to regulate it,
The new dark age exposes us to more nightmares,
The island of ignorance stands between black seas,
In the infinite one can flee from the deadly to peace,
The fears of the past are rewritten looking for changes,
The negative are lessons to learn to unlearn,
Wild nature is the dogma of visualizing Magic,
The madness of knowing everything is the prison for not existing,
Every moral compass looks at the vertigo of the horror of gods,
The simulation of who we are is a passing sum,
The human machine is a hidden side of the game called life,
Between punishments and rewards dreams are forgotten,
Constant changes are the evolutionary line knew.

156   The Endless Wait

Someone finds a design where a cycle begins,
A belt wraps bitterness with limited joys,
A diverse polarization is divided into two little boxes,
The passengers of history live in the illusion of deciding,
A reboot is born in sympathy with the ashes of the system,
In politics two truths are hidden between a lie,
Promises without responsibilities are worthless
The models of comparison are ideologies with judgments,
Equal paths bring much inequality,
The illusion in time hides trips in insecurity,
The oppressed existence surrounds a passing bubble,
Humans turned into tools for needs,
Society is used for functional objectives,
Various genocides turn people into numbers,
The mirror of fear turns blind attempts into resources,
The testimonies lose value before the political truths,
Hypocrisy traps the emptiness of the present deserter,
The origin of the communication is processed with speed,
Always connected creates an uncertainty to consumption,
Disconnect becomes an inhuman line,
Empathy forms a movie of passing comfort,
Survivors looking for reasons that separate happiness,
Working for freedom momentary pleasures are tied,
An embrace of evolution intersects with fear of elections,
The new philosophy unites the moral to be independent,
A simple doll rests in the reason of ties,
The rules condemn the emptiness of heaven and hell,
Upon leaving the mask a giant octopus stalks the way,
The era of insecurity in the hands of the invisible wait.

157 The Wagon of Love

A train goes through the stations of destiny,
In some beginning learning begins before love,
Between beginnings and endings hearts are not heard,
There are some crossroads where bells ring
Some passengers pass by because they forget to get off,
Infinite mirrors send reflections without being perceived,
In some unions, being kind is allowed to escape,
Running through the image the whirlpool catches us,
The gift of connection is opened by not looking at targets,
There are brilliant ones that take away the energy to seek interests,
Other glitters reflect the stars to accompany you,
There are appearances that use the current for relief,
Taking a breath no one can be all you want
Filling something completely leaves no room for emptiness.
A constant balance is found in adding something every day,
Conflicts meet with hope for changes,
In criticism lies the secret of the enemy himself,
Each one offers what exists within his heart,
He who appreciates what surrounds him is loaded with blessings,
Boundless intentions have courage to give joy,
The wounds of childhood are repeated in relationships,
When feeling rejection, isolations come with escapes,
When feeling abandoned, they try to catch the couple,
When feeling humiliation, shame saves pain to help,
When feeling betrayals, resistance is to impose rules,
Feeling injustice requires doing much to seek appreciation,
For some people you will be light for others darkness,
The choice is to look for the one who adds you, not the one who
subtracts you,
The eternal meeting of souls already has its destiny written.

The refuge of the fugitive gets bigger and bigger,
Mistrust becomes a race that governs,
Some traps catch prey in emotional pain,
Marketing lodges demand exuberant profiles,
Some lights go out to isolate time in moments,
The siren calls return to seek revenge,
The thoughts do not stop in the silence of relief,
Complaints return to continue in distracted ceremonies,
Turbulences become distractions in the novel,
The costs of power keep trying to do and convince,
Bets become unlimited behind the goal,
Some defeats are blocked to follow more paths,
Patience is very limited to move on to the next oblivion,
The pages slide with speed of a second,
The looks are the owners of the image, not the content,
In search of identities, feelings are forgotten,
The songs howl in expectation of resources for interests,
Moments are paralyzed when the demanding shortage arrives,
The always open store does not remember the previous purchase,
Borders are easily crossed as long as there are benefits,
When visualizing inequality, protective walls are erected,
Around a corner awaits the desert that submerges,
The tunnel door keeps time with worn traces,
The conquering fights consume the last resources,
Advertising creates vulnerable bursts of hope,
Some bubbles are dangerous traps with scars,
A few explosions are contaminating the art of living,
Lamenting the search for peace, values are lost,
Wandering in the void, a rock is built in the heart.

159 Mother Teresa of Calcutta

A traveler of hugs says that she rests in LOVE,
Humans place is where his brother needs them,
The call of need is not denied help,
You don't let anyone walk away from you without being a little happier,
Be faithful to the little things because strength lives in them,
Kind words have echoes hard to forget,
The Joy of the heart is the magnet that indicates the way,
A small impact of support transcends into more actions,
People come as blessings others as lessons
Discipline is the bridge between goals and achievements,
Nature grows and moves silently with freedom,
The most beautiful day is today and the easiest thing is to make a mistake,
Fear is a big obstacle and the biggest mistake is abandoning yourself,
The root of all evil is selfishness and greed,
The best teachers for balance are children,
The most dangerous person is the liar and base,
The most beautiful gift is forgiveness and the most united is the home,
The most powerful force is faith and fulfillment peace,
The most important things are parents like shelter,
Reaching knowledge brings us closer to divine rest,
Calm thoughts so that sounds guide your dreams,
The spirit is the duster to clean any cobwebs,
The eyes are the windows where Christ enters the heart,
If you don't know how to serve, you can't know how to live with dignity.
Together great things can be done from wisdom,
Alchemy awaits the transformation of stone and metal,
Equally rich and poor receive the stellar fragrance,
With sweet breath life looks at destiny towards the sky,
Obey those who teach more than those who rule.